D1569709

Advance Praise for

Addressing Parental Accommodation

When Treating Anxiety in Children

"It's all about accommodation, and Lebowitz does an impressive job describing (a) accommodation and all its feature and (b) the application of strategies designed to reduce parent accommodation. Unburdened by excessive citations, yet rich with case descriptions, this well-informed and readable work recognizes that prior parent interventions for child anxiety were typically added-on to child treatment, rather than being an independent stand-alone approach. Lebowitz provides an excellent resource for those wanting to learn about changing parent accommodation to favorably impact child anxiety and OCD."

—**Philip C. Kendall, PhD, ABPP**, Distinguished University Professor, Laura H. Carnell Professor of Psychology, Temple University

"Eli Lebowitz scores big with this innovative, highly readable, and practical guide for therapists who work with anxious children and their families. Unlike many standard child-focused treatments for anxious children, this approach is oriented towards working primarily with and through *parents* who inadvertently or otherwise accommodate the very fears and anxieties they wish to change in their children. This is not to say the parents *cause* the fear and anxiety; rather, and most importantly, it acknowledges the role that parents play in accommodating and perhaps maintaining these fears and anxieties. Far too many children do not benefit from our standard child-focused treatments and we simply must do more to enhance the effectiveness and reach of our interventions. Here, Lebowitz presents us with a developmentally-sensitive, contextually-informed, and evidence-based approach which will help us address the weaknesses in our extant approaches. It is a volume whose time has surely come."

—**Thomas H. Ollendick, PhD**, University Distinguished Professor, Director, Child Study Center, Virginia Tech

ABCT Clinical Practice Series

Series Editor

Susan W. White, PhD, ABPP, Professor and Doddridge Saxon Chair in Clinical Psychology, University of Alabama

Associate Editors

Lara J. Farrell, PhD, Associate Professor, School of Applied Psychology, Griffith University, and Menzies Health Institute of Queensland, Australia

Matthew A. Jarrett, PhD, Associate Professor, Department of Psychology, University of Alabama

Jordana Muroff, PhD, LICSW, Associate Professor, Clinical Practice, Boston University School of Social Work

Marisol Perez, PhD, Associate Professor & Associate Chair, Department of Psychology, Arizona State University

Titles in the Series

Applications of the Unified Protocol for Transdiagnostic Treatment of Emotional Disorders
Edited by David H. Barlow and Todd Farchione

Helping Families of Youth with School Attendance Problems
Christopher A. Kearney

Forthcoming titles in the series

Conducting Exposure with Children and Adolescents
Stephen P. Whiteside and Thomas H. Ollendick

Addressing Parental Accommodation When Treating Anxiety in Children

ELI R. LEBOWITZ

OXFORD
UNIVERSITY PRESS

OXFORD
UNIVERSITY PRESS

Oxford University Press is a department of the University of Oxford. It furthers
the University's objective of excellence in research, scholarship, and education
by publishing worldwide. Oxford is a registered trade mark of Oxford University
Press in the UK and certain other countries.

Published in the United States of America by Oxford University Press
198 Madison Avenue, New York, NY 10016, United States of America.

Library of Congress Cataloging-in-Publication Data
Names: Lebowitz, Eli R., author.
Title: Addressing parental accommodation when treating anxiety in children /
by Eli R. Lebowitz.
Description: New York : Oxford University Press, [2019] |
Series: ABCT clinical practice series | Includes bibliographical references and index.
Identifiers: LCCN 2019004683 (print) | LCCN 2019013563 (ebook) |
ISBN 9780190869991 (UPDF) | ISBN 9780190870003 (EPUB) |
ISBN 9780190869984 (pbk. : alk. paper)
Subjects: LCSH: Anxiety in children. | Anxiety—Treatment. | Adjustment (Psychology)
Classification: LCC BF723.A5 (ebook) | LCC BF723.A5 L392 2019 (print) | DDC 155.4/1246—dc23
LC record available at https://lccn.loc.gov/2019004683

CONTENTS

**SECTION 5 Case Examples: Addressing Family Accommodation
As Stand-Alone Treatment**

SERIES FOREWORD

Mental health clinicians desperately want to help their clients and recognize the importance of implementing evidence-based treatments toward achieving this goal. In the past several years, the field of mental healthcare has seen tremendous advances in our understanding of pathology and its underlying mechanisms, as well as proliferation and refinement of scientifically informed treatment approaches. Coinciding with these advances is a heightened focus on accountability in clinical practice. Clinicians are expected to apply evidence-based approaches and to do so effectively, efficiently, and in a patient-centered, individualized way. This is no small order. For a multitude of reasons, including but not limited to client diversity, complex psychopathology (e.g., comorbidity), and barriers to care that are not under the clinician's control (e.g., adverse life circumstances that limit the client's ability to participate), delivery of evidence-based approaches can be challenging.

This series, which represents a collaborative effort between the Association for Behavioral and Cognitive Therapies (ABCT) and the Oxford University Press, is intended to serve as an easy-to-use, highly practical collection of resources for clinicians and trainees. The ABCT Clinical Practice Series is designed to help clinicians effectively master and implement evidence-based treatment approaches. In practical terms, the series represents the "brass tacks" of implementation, including basic how-to guidance and advice on troubleshooting common issues in clinical practice and application. As such, the series is best viewed as a complement to other series on evidence-based protocols such as the Treatments That Work™ series and the Programs That Work™ series. These represent seminal bridges between research and practice and have been instrumental in the dissemination of empirically supported intervention protocols and programs. The ABCT Clinical Practice Series, rather than focusing on specific diagnoses and their treatment, targets the practical application of therapeutic and assessment approaches. In other words, the emphasis is on the *how-to* aspects of mental health delivery.

It is my hope that clinicians and trainees find these books useful in refining their clinical skills, as enhanced comfort as well as competence in delivery of evidence-based approaches should ultimately lead to improved client outcomes. Given the emphasis on application in this series, there is relatively less emphasis on review of the underlying research base. Readers who wish to delve more deeply into the theoretical or empirical basis supporting specific approaches are encouraged to go to the original source publications cited in each chapter. When relevant, suggestions for further reading are provided.

Anxious children often have parents who hate to see their child endure such duress and, understandably, take measures to help their child feel better. Clinicians have long recognized this phenomenon and the unintended adverse consequences of such parental behaviors. Although other resources and several treatment manuals for childhood anxiety include suggestions for managing parent behaviors that unwittingly undermine therapists' attempts to reduce anxiety, this is the first book to focus specifically on how to address family accommodation. Dr. Eli Lebowitz, the world's foremost expert on managing parental accommodation therapeutically, provides the "how to" information needed to identify and reduce accommodating behaviors. Accommodation in this context refers to the behaviors parents engage in to help their child experience less distress and anxiety. As most clinicians who work with children know first-hand, if parental accommodation is not addressed and minimized, its presence will dampen therapeutic effectiveness.

This book provides the necessary theoretical and conceptual framework for the reader to understand what accommodation is, including how it can present, the mechanisms or functions of accommodation, and the research evidence for the import of reducing its presence during treatment. The bulk of this book is dedicated to the application of strategies designed to reduce accommodation. Supplemented by detailed strategies and case examples as well as clinically informed approaches for how to plan for (and overcome) common obstacles, this book will surely be a valuable resource for clinicians who work with anxious children and their parents.

Susan W. White, PhD, ABPP
Series Editor

ABOUT THE AUTHOR

Professor Lebowitz studies and treats childhood and adolescent anxiety at the Yale School of Medicine, Child Study Center, where he directs the Program for Anxiety Disorders. His research focuses on the development, neurobiology, and treatment of anxiety and related disorders, with special emphasis on family dynamics and the role of parents in these disorders. Dr. Lebowitz is the lead investigator on multiple funded research projects, and is the author of research papers, books and chapters on childhood and adolescent anxiety. Dr. Lebowitz' work has been recognized by private and public organizations including the Brain and Behavior Foundation, the National Institute of Mental Health and The National Center for Advancing Translational Science. He is also the father of three great boys.

Addressing Parental Accommodation
When Treating Anxiety in Children

Family Accommodation

How, What, and Why

Introduction to Accommodation of Child Anxiety

Family accommodation of childhood anxiety is the term used to describe the myriad changes that parents and other family members make to their behaviors and living patterns due to a child's anxiety disorder. Parenting a child with any psychological disorder, or, indeed, with any medical or emotional condition, almost inevitably will lead to changes in parental behavior. But families of children with heightened vulnerability to anxiety and its disorders are particularly susceptible to the familial impact of their child's difficulty, and accommodation of childhood anxiety is special and different from accommodation of other mental and physical problems. Children rely instinctively on parents for help in coping with anxiety, and parents are naturally attuned to fear and anxiety cues displayed by their children. This natural pattern of children relying on parental figures to alleviate anxiety and of parental motivation to "step-in" and provide protection and reassurance when a child is anxious sets the stage for the extremely high prevalence of family accommodation observed among families of anxious children. Moreover, while accommodation can be necessary and helpful in coping with many physical and emotional conditions, accommodation of childhood anxiety will usually have a negative impact in the long term, leading to increased anxiety over time. A key difference between accommodation of anxiety and of other problems is that independent coping is key to overcoming anxiety. Whereas a child with a physical disability may require accommodations to maximize their potential and be able to achieve on an even playing field with others who do not have the same problem, a child with anxiety will often require the opposite. By accommodating to the child's anxiety symptoms, the likelihood of the child fulfilling their potential can actually be reduced. Of course, not all accommodation is detrimental, and this book provides useful guidelines for differentiating between helpful and nonhelpful accommodations. A rule of thumb for helping to make this distinction is that accommodations that help a child to gradually cope more independently, to increase functioning, and to lessen avoidance are usually helpful. In contrast, accommodations that help a child to avoid more, to reduce their independent functioning, or to become more dependent on parents or others are likely to be unhelpful over time.

It is also useful to note at this point that this book deals with the treatment of children with anxiety disorders whose daily functioning has been impaired by anxiety over a significant period of time. Many of the principles and tools described in the book apply well to children who are experiencing more normative or transient anxiety, and, indeed, application of these tools and principles may be useful in preventing the development of a more clinically impairing anxiety disorder. However, in the same way that it does not make sense to treat every manifestation of fearful avoidance as a problem or as a symptom to be vigorously addressed, it also does not make sense to see every accommodation of a child's fear or anxiety as symptomatic of a larger problem or as a target for emphatic intervention. Every child will experience anxiety some of the time and while encouraging coping and refraining from accommodation is generally good advice, a healthy child who is not predisposed to more serious anxiety is unlikely to be harmed by parents' natural inclination to accommodation or protective responses.

Research in recent years, conducted in large samples of parents of clinically anxious children from numerous locations around the world and with a variety of cultural and ethnic backgrounds, demonstrates that family accommodation of child anxiety is the rule and not exception. The preponderance of data from these studies point to the conclusion that, when coping with an anxious child, almost all parents engage in frequent accommodation of their child's symptoms. This chapter provides an overview of some of the common ways in which anxious children are accommodated, focusing first on parents and then on others within, and even outside of, the family circle. The chapter then describes some of the key factors that drive these patterns of accommodation, including the desire to avoid or reduce a child's suffering; common misconceptions about anxiety held by many parents (and sometimes reinforced by well-meaning but ultimately misguided providers); the need to facilitate functional goals for the child, parent, and family; and forceful demands for accommodation that are frequently made by the child.

WHAT IS ACCOMMODATION

Family accommodation can take an infinite variety of forms, and clinicians working with anxious children and their families can usually recount many different examples of the accommodations they have encountered in their work. Just as there is no particular limit to the variety of stimuli that children can fear or to the situations they may avoid due to anxiety or to the content of the worried thoughts that plague anxious children, there is also no end to the ways in which those who love and care for anxious children may accommodate the child's anxiety.

Family accommodation is conceptualized as a *response* to child anxiety (distinct from, although not unrelated to, parental styles or traits that may precipitate child anxiety, which are also discussed in this chapter). The simplest rule of thumb for describing the variety in family accommodation is a paraphrasing of Newton's third law: *For every child anxiety symptom, there is an equal accommodation of the child's anxiety.* Of course, not every parent will accommodate equally, and not every symptom a given child exhibits will elicit the same degree of accommodation, even in the same parent, but the potential to accommodate is no more limited than the child's anxiety symptoms themselves.

Yet, just as with the symptoms of child anxiety, some accommodations are more common than others. Research dating back to the 1970s indicated that evolutionary predispositions and environmental factors contribute to the nonrandom distribution of fears in the population (Seligman, 1971). Fears of separation, the dark, animals, natural phenomena, and social evaluation and fears relating to the intense physical and psychological manifestations of anxiety itself, to cite a few prominent examples, are more common than fears of guns, electrical outlets, or cars, although these are all present in the environment and pose larger realistic threats to children's safety and well-being. In similar fashion, through rich clinical experience and intense empirical research over recent years, predictable patterns of accommodation emerge, helping to guide the work of clinicians engaged in assessing or intervening with families of anxious children (Benito et al., 2015; Lebowitz, Panza, & Bloch, 2016; Lebowitz, Scharfstein, & Jones, 2014, 2015; Reuman & Abramowitz, 2017; Settipani, 2015; Storch et al., 2015; Thompson-Hollands, Kerns, Pincus, & Comer, 2014).

Two useful ways of organizing the tremendous variety in family accommodation are to categorize accommodations either by the *form* the accommodation takes or by the *domain* of child anxiety being accommodated. Several studies, building on work done originally in studying family accommodation of obsessive-compulsive disorder (OCD; Calvocoressi et al., 1995), have demonstrated the utility of dividing accommodation into two main forms: participation in anxiety-driven behaviors and modification of family routines and schedules. Table 1.1 categorizes some common accommodations based on form of accommodation and domain of child anxiety.

PARTICIPATION AND MODIFICATION

Participation

Parents who repeatedly check the homework of a child who is anxious and perfectionistic or accompany their child to class parties and stay for the duration of the event or stay in the bathroom while their child is showering or bring water bottles to every out-of-home excursion because their child fears being without them in case panic symptoms occur or sleep next to their child because of separation anxiety can all be thought of as accommodating by participating in anxiety-driven behaviors. Many parents become adept at anticipating their child's anxious responses and will act preemptively, forestalling the difficult situation through

Table 1.1 Examples of Family Accommodations Organized by Domain of Child Anxiety and by Form of Accommodation (Participation and Modification)

	Separation	Social	OCD	Panic	Generalized	Phobias
Participation	Sleeping in child's bed	Answering questions in place of child	Washing hands with child supervision	Taking child to doctor visits or emergency room	Providing repeated reassurance	Not saying the word *snake*
	Responding to many phone calls each day	Speaking softly in public	Providing extra soap	Accompanying child places	Providing detailed schedules	Checking whether forecast repeatedly
	Not closing bathroom door when showering	Asking teachers not to call on child	Wearing special clothes	Carrying water bottles or other "emergency" equipment	Checking homework repeatedly	Not staying out after dark
	Walking child into school each morning	Rushing home to avoid public bathroom	Listen to child's "confessions"		Providing detailed information about the family finances or health	Taking stairs instead of elevator
	Accompanying child in to the bathroom	Ordering for child in restaurants	Carrying child physically		Answering repeated questions	
		Asking teachers for help in place of child			Planning child's outfits for entire week ahead of time	

Modification					
Refraining from work trips	Not going to restaurants	Keeping windows closed	Coming home early from work	Avoiding changes to routines or schedules	Planning outings and vacation to avoid feared stimuli
Not going out in the evening	Avoiding social gatherings	Avoiding "contaminated" places	Picking up child early from school because of panic symptoms	Leaving early to make sure child is never late	Keeping lights on at night
Stay with child at after school activities or parties	Driving child to school instead of using school bus	Providing special foods or meals	Avoiding places where panic attacks have occurred	Staying up late with child at night	Not visiting friends with dogs
	Avoiding malls	Driving special routes to avoid avoiding certain roads			Not taking child for shots or doctor visits
		Being late to work because of waiting for child to complete rituals			Driving places instead of flying

their accommodation, as when a parent swiftly replies to a question posed to a socially anxious child.

In other cases, participation can occur when parents refrain from certain behaviors they know are likely to trigger their child's anxiety. In other words, participation can be a passive, as well as an active, behavior. For example, when parents make sure not to have the news on television when their child is in the room because they know the child is prone to becoming anxious at reports about international conflicts, health concerns, or the economy. Other parents may refrain from using "trigger words" that make their child anxious or avoid opening windows at home because their child has a fear of insects or in the car because their child becomes distraught at the thought that others might hear them speaking.

Modifications

Family life can often appear to be organized around a child's anxiety to a surprising degree. Mealtimes, work schedules, travel plans, bedtime routines, transportation choices, and leisure activities can all be shaped by the perceived need to steer clear of an anxious child's symptoms. For example, parents may drive needlessly long routes that avoid freeways because of a child who becomes nervous and fears accidents or traffic. Or they may leave the house earlier than necessary because the child is fearful of being late. Parents frequently return home from work earlier than they otherwise might because a child is distressed if they are not home before dark or if they must remain home alone. Parents often plan the day's activities down to the minute because a child is uncomfortable with any uncertainty in the schedule and may provide detailed information about the plans to the child (an example of participation). Many children have fears relating to food and eating, and these can cause significant disruption to mealtime routines. One parent may become solely responsible for preparing food because otherwise the child is anxious or avoids eating, or meals may be held at rigidly determined times because variation in the schedule causes upheaval and stress. When a child is afraid of insects, family outings may be modified to exclude picnics or nature, or if the child is uncomfortable in closed or crowded places, the family may avoid going to movies or malls.

There is no firm boundary between participations and modifications, and many of these accommodations may be viewed as representing one or the other, or both of these categories. But empirical data support the construct validity of these two modes of accommodation, and clinical research supports the usefulness of the complementary and overlapping categories of participation and modification in creating a structure for mapping out and identifying a family's accommodations. Thoroughly assessing accommodation in the evaluation of child anxiety and in treatment planning is highly valuable and will be discussed in depth in a later chapter.

DOMAINS OF ANXIETY

Another useful way of organizing the variety of accommodations encountered in clinical work, and even within a given family, is in relation to the domains of anxiety experienced by the child. Studies of childhood anxiety disorder consistently report that comorbidity between the anxiety disorders is very high, meaning that most children presenting for treatment with an anxiety disorder will actually meet diagnostic criteria for at least one, and often several, other comorbid anxiety disorders. There is often a chief presenting complaint that serves as the impetus for the family seeking professional help, but savvy clinicians know not to begin treatment before also assessing for additional anxiety problems. The current DSM-5 and ICD-10 nosologies classify anxiety disorders based primarily on the situations or stimuli that trigger excessive or inappropriate anxiety. Thus, a child who is fearful at the prospect of separation from primary attachment figures is classified as having separation anxiety disorder, a child who is concerned with negative evaluation and avoids social situations is described as having social phobia, and so forth. These distinctions are useful in capturing a child's symptoms and facilitate productive assessment procedures, but they do not account for the shared underlying pathophysiology in neural circuitry and endocrinology, the genetic and nongenetic heritability of anxiety vulnerability, and the phenomenology that are common across the different anxiety disorders. Hypervigilance, deficits in self-regulation, predisposition to negative affectivity, and other functional and biological constructs cut across the anxiety disorders, contributing to the high co-occurrence of these disorders in children as well adults.

Each domain of elevated anxiety present in a child is typically going to be paralleled by family accommodations. And, like the child's symptoms, some of which will relate to a particular domain of anxiety while others will relate more broadly to multiple domains, the accommodations will also be partly specific to particular domains and partly broadly relevant to a variety of domains. Categorizing the accommodations in relation to the domains of anxiety they help to avoid or alleviate can help to make sense of the many accommodations encountered by the clinician and facilitates assessment and treatment planning. An exhaustive list of possible accommodations is, of course, impossible. There follow some examples of frequently reported accommodations, organized by domains of common childhood anxiety disorders.

Generalized Anxiety

Children with generalized anxiety experience chronic and exhausting worry that interferes with physical and emotional well-being, disrupts age-appropriate functioning, and causes marked personal distress. The most common form of accommodation for children with generalized anxiety is the provision of repeated reassurance about their worries and concerns. Children with generalized anxiety seek reassurance through endless questions, often repeating the same questions many times over. Parents accommodate by replying to these questions, often "promising" or "swearing" that a feared event will not occur. In some cases, parents will engage in additional behaviors aimed at instilling confidence in a child that a catastrophizing thought is exaggerated and does not reflect a realistic threat assessment.

> *Mason was 11 years old and was constantly preoccupied with the possibility that his father, who smoked, would become seriously ill. Mason imagined his father having a heart attack and dying on the way to the hospital. Mason's father, Liam, repeatedly reassured him that he was healthy and had even taken Mason with him to an annual physical so he could hear the doctor pronounce him in good health, but Liam continued to be worried that the doctor "may have missed something." One morning, an exasperated Liam got on the family's treadmill and told Mason, "Watch, I'm going to run a mile and you'll see that my heart is just fine." Mason was relieved when his father completed the mile and was hardly winded at all. The next morning as Liam was preparing to leave for work Mason asked him to run the mile again. An amused Liam acquiesced and ran a mile with Mason watching closely. Liam's amusement was soon replaced with frustration as Mason began demanding to see his father run a mile every morning, in what soon became a new morning routine. Liam joked to the therapist that he was "now more fit than ever," but was unsure how to stop the often-inconvenient routine. Mason became tearful and whiny if Liam attempted to leave the house without "doing the mile" under Mason's supervision.*

Generalized anxiety can also lead to other common forms of accommodation. Medical concerns can apply to the child themselves, as well as to loved ones, and the chronic stress of generalized anxiety contribute to actual somatic complaints in many children. Parents may find themselves taking children to unnecessary doctor appointments, providing "placebo" medications (such as vitamins that are given to reassure the child, rather than as a parental health choice), or staying home with a child who feels unwell in the morning after a restless night. Because many worries surface around bedtime, parents will often report engaging in lengthy nighttime rituals, at the expense of other activities and responsibilities.

Many parents accommodate by helping their child to avoid doubts about school work or grades, checking and rechecking work, sometimes late into the night. And because children with generalized anxiety are often highly sensitive to uncertainty and averse to change, family routines are often planned out to an excessive degree and rigidly adhered to, even when causing inconvenience. Children may demand to know in advance who will pick them up from school or what the weekend plans will be in detail, and they may react negatively to any deviation from the stated plans. And new activities, such as going skiing for the first time or traveling to a new destination, may be avoided because the child becomes overwhelmed when confronting a new experience. As a result, the child may be exposed to fewer activities and less stimulation, because the parents are apprehensive about enrolling them in extracurricular activities or sports.

Worries relating to family issues such as the parents' relationship or the family's finances can lead to other accommodations. Parents may feel they are tiptoeing around such issues. One example is feeling afraid to label a purchase as expensive or costly because their child interprets such statements as a sign that they do not have enough money and may soon experience poverty or homelessness.

Social Phobia

Children with social phobia fear being negatively evaluated by others and will avoid social situations that carry the potential for judgement or evaluation, or the child will endure such situations with considerable distress. Accommodation of socially anxious children often centers around two main points: helping the child to avoid social situations and interacting with others on the child's behalf. Parents may engage teachers and school staff in the accommodation in ways such as asking teachers not to call on a child in class, requesting that the child be excused from oral presentations and assignments, or keeping the child home on days with presentations. Parents may also take phone calls in place of the child, "warn" the child when guests are coming to the home, refrain from going (or taking the child) to social encounters such as family gatherings or religious services, or otherwise help the child to avoid social encounters. During social situations, parents (or siblings) commonly speak in place of the child. For example, parents may place a child's order in a restaurant, speak to a store clerk on behalf the child, or answer questions posed by friends, relatives, or others. The parent may feel compelled to accommodate the child because of the child's distress and anxiety, but the parent's own embarrassment about the child's behavior can also contribute to the accommodation. The silence that ensues when a socially anxious child does not answer a question or greeting can feel like eternity, placing pressure on the parent to intervene. Selective mutism is closely related to social phobia and will often be accompanied by the same kinds of accommodations, in particular speaking in place of the child.

> *Janet always kept her daughter Paisley home on the first day of each school year and would bring her to school on the second day. Janet explained that the first day "always has lots of introductions and role calling," and she knew it would be extra hard for Paisley. "It's just easier for her to start on day two and just kind of slip into things."*

Separation Anxiety

Children with separation anxiety fear being separated from parents, try to avoid separations, and react to separation with distress including crying or physically

clinging to the parent. Not surprisingly, parents of children with separation anxiety usually find themselves engaging in high levels of accommodation. Indeed,
the nature of separation anxiety, with the inherent dependence on parental proximity, makes it difficult to imagine a child having separation anxiety without some
significant degree of accommodation on the parents' side. Because anxiety of almost any kind can be reduced in a child through proximity to a parent, children
who are anxious about different things will often present with separation anxiety. For example, a child who is worried about their health (a symptom commonly associated with generalized anxiety) may show symptoms of separation
anxiety because being close to their parent helps alleviate their worry, while being
alone intensifies them. In this sense, almost all anxiety in children is also "separation anxiety" and can lead to accommodation in the separation anxiety domain.
Parents of children with separation anxiety will frequently stay near them when in
the home, for example, letting them know when they are moving to another room
so the child can follow, keeping doors open so the child can maintain eye contact
with them (sometimes even while the parent or child is using the bathroom),
accompanying the child when the child must go to another room (e.g., when a
child wants to go upstairs and get a game or a book), and refraining from sending
the child to areas of the house away from the parent (e.g., not asking the child to
go to the basement or attic).

Other common forms of accommodation in separation anxiety include limiting parental absences from home, maintaining contact over phone calls or texts
during separations, limiting child outings without the parent, and being near the
child during the night. Parents often limit their own absences from the house, either returning earlier than they otherwise would or not going out when the child
is home. Many parents of children with separation anxiety will avoid both parents
going out at the same time during the afternoon or evening, ensuring that at least
one parent stays home with the child rather than engaging a babysitter (or leaving
the child alone or with siblings when appropriate). Parents may also report that
they inform the child ahead of time of even the smallest separations or regularly
have to promise the child that no separation is planned. They may also accompany
the child to places and events that a child would normally attend alone. This could
include staying at school together with the child during school hours, going with
them to peer parties, staying to wait during extracurriculars such as sport practice or art or music classes, always volunteering to host sleepovers so the child
does not face sleeping at another child's home, and waiting to leave for work until
the child has been picked up by the school bus, among countless other examples.
In many cases the parent will accommodate separation anxiety by helping the
child to maintain contact with them during periods of separation. Responding to
frequent phone calls, video chats, or text messages, even while at work or while
a child is in school (or both) is not uncommon. One parent described waiting
outside his child's school at least 30 minutes before the end of each school day
because his daughter was so anxious that he would not be there on time and she
would be left alone.

Nighttime, with its opportunity for lengthy separation and hours of darkness, is often a time of elevated separation anxiety and, correspondingly, high family accommodation. Parents of children with separation anxiety often sleep next to their child, whether in the child's bed or in their own, or remain with the child until the child has fallen asleep before leaving them alone. A child with separation anxiety may rely on a lengthy nighttime ritual, sometimes including countless repetitions of particular comforting phrases or endless hugs and kisses, which can be time-consuming and frustrating for the parent. Even after falling asleep, many children with separation anxiety will wake up during the night and either come to or call their parents, and the lengthy cycle of bedtime rituals may be repeated all over again before the child falls back asleep.

Julian and Hazel felt like they no longer had any life of their own. Their son Connor was nine years old, and it seemed like they never had a moment away from him. "He's either in school or he's with us," explained Hazel. "And I don't just mean at home with us. I mean literally WITH us. Like on top of us. If we try to leave a room he's in, you would think he was being murdered! He'll scream, in a panic, with terror in his eyes. So of course, we never leave him alone. He'll only go to the bathroom without us if he can get his little brother to go sit in there with him. We know it's crazy, but it seems like the times he's in the bathroom with this brother are the only times we get to be just the two of us!" Julian added: "I used to feel like at least at work I can be focused on something else. Now even when I'm at work I'm either answering his calls, talking to him on FaceTime, or replying to his text messages. Yesterday he texted me 38 times!"

Specific Phobias

Children with specific phobias experience extreme and irrational fears of a particular object, animal, or situation. They will try to avoid exposure to the feared stimulus and will respond with fear and distress to potential or actual need to confront it. The accommodations to specific phobias are as varied as the possible phobias themselves but will generally entail some facilitation of the child's avoidance of the phobic stimulus or situation. When a child fears dogs, for example, parents may avoid visiting homes or places with dogs or may even refrain from watching movies or shows that feature dogs. A friend of the author recently recounted a personal anecdote in which after being invited to visit some family friends, the invitation was sheepishly and apologetically rescinded by the hosts because their child knew that they owned a dog and was scared of the visit despite there being no intent to bring the dog along! Parents of children with fears of insects may avoid excursions to nature or keep windows shut in the summer; parents of children with fears of heights may avoid visiting certain destinations or driving over bridges; and parents of children with fears of storms may keep a child home from school during bad weather or provide excessive amounts of reassurance about possible storms. One parent described becoming a "weather channel junky" just to be able to answer all her child's weather-related questions each day.

> *Piper was 14 years old and for several years had suffered from a severe phobia of needles and doctors. Her parents had not been able to get her to the doctor for check-ups or vaccinations, her teeth required urgent attention, and her school, which already excluded her from certain activities because of not having a health report, was now threatening not to allow Piper to attend school at all unless she saw a doctor. "But the straw that broke the camel's back," described Piper's parents, "was that she is now demanding that her sister not go to the doctor either. We thought the problem would be that her sister would develop a fear as well just from listening to her carry on, but fortunately she seems fine with it. Piper, however, is now saying she can't cope with anyone in the family going near a doctor. When we realized we were making plans to lie to her about where her sister was going we realized we're in trouble. We need help!"*

Panic and Agoraphobia

Children with panic disorder experience recurring unexpected panic attacks, or sudden surges in fear and anxiety, and become concerned with the possibility of additional attacks. Children with the closely related agoraphobia are fearful of developing panic symptoms in situations from which it would be hard to escape, such as public transportation or closed (or wide-open) spaces, and try to avoid those situations, especially when alone. Parents of children with panic and agoraphobia typically accommodate by either accompanying the child when they fear they will experience panic symptoms or facilitating the child's avoidance of the feared situations, as well as by providing reassurance about the child's physical health. Parents may request that a child be exempt from physical education in school because the child is afraid that exercise will trigger a panic attack. Or parents may drive the child to school each day because the child is afraid of having panic symptoms on the bus, not being able to escape, and being socially embarrassed or humiliated in front of peers. Frequently, parents will accompany the child to places the child would otherwise go alone. For example, driving a teenager to the mall because the teen is afraid to drive themselves or regularly volunteering to chaperone school outings because the child is nervous about being away from parents in case of a panic attack. In addition to avoiding being alone, many children with panic and agoraphobia will engage in other safety behaviors because of the fear of panic, and parents may accommodate by providing safety items or otherwise maintaining the safety behavior. Talking to a child on the phone when they are worried about having panic symptoms and always carrying antianxiety medication, water, or an inhaler are examples of safety behaviors that parents may be accommodating.

"After Miguel's first panic attack we were all so scared," recall Alejandro and Lydia. "We thought he was very sick, and it was a big relief to learn it was just anxiety. But Miguel didn't see it that way. He says we can't understand how awful it feels to have a panic attack, and he's right. We can't really understand, but we know we want to help him never feel so bad again. We actually moved so he could walk to school in the morning and not have to ride the bus, where he says he's sure to have a panic attack. And a lot of times we have to leave events early because he starts to feel panicky. It's not convenient, but it's worth it to us."

Obsessive-Compulsive Disorder

The DSM-5, published in 2013, no longer classifies OCD as an anxiety disorder but continues to recognize the tight link between OCD and anxiety. For many intents and purposes, including with regards to family accommodation, OCD can still be thought of as an anxiety disorder. Indeed, research indicates a high degree of similarity in the prevalence and frequency of family accommodation in OCD and the other childhood anxiety disorders. Children with OCD experience intrusive thoughts and urges that cause them anxiety and distress and feel compelled to maintain rigid rules and rituals that can be time-consuming and interfering. Children with OCD usually have insight into the unrealistic nature of their thoughts and the irrational nature of their rituals but feel unable to control them. Family accommodation was studied initially in OCD (first in adults and then in children) and is as common in OCD as in other anxiety disorders. Parents of children with OCD often actively participate in rituals. These include performing repeated checks together with or on behalf of the child, listening to the child's ritualized "confessions," performing cleaning rituals such as excessive handwashing, and providing items that the child needs for the completion of their rituals such as buying extra soap or toilet paper. Parents also accommodate by providing reassurance about the thoughts, answering compulsive questions, making choices for a child who is compulsively doubtful and indecisive, avoiding the use of "special numbers" that have taken on a negative connotation in the child's mind (e.g., only serving the child multiples of threes of any particular food item). Other obsessive-compulsive-related disorders are also commonly accommodated. Parents of a child with pathological hoarding, for example, may refrain from entering the child's room or cleaning it, may agree not to throw things away, and may even save useless (or even offensive) items that the child feels compelled to keep. And parents of a child with a body dysmorphic disorder may take them to doctors, provide endless reassurance, or even allow them to undergo unnecessary medical procedures to correct a perceived flaw or imperfection.

ACCOMMODATION AND RELATED
PARENTING BEHAVIOR

Many studies have examined possible links between parental behaviors, styles, and traits and anxiety and its disorders in children (Bögels & Brechman-Toussaint, 2006; Ginsburg, Siqueland, Masia-Warner, & Hedtke, 2004; Wood, McLeod, Sigman, Hwang, & Chu, 2003). While such links have frequently been reported, research in this area has notable limitations, and it is easy to overstate the actual evidence for the role of parental characteristics in the etiology, maintenance, or course of childhood anxiety. Most of the research examining parental behaviors and childhood anxiety outcomes has relied on cross-sectional data. That is to say, rather than examining parental behaviors in new or expecting parents and then following those families to observe which parents had children with anxiety disorders (longitudinal research), parents of children with anxiety disorders and parents of children without anxiety disorders are compared at a single time point and differences between the two groups are presumed to be linked to the phenomenon of child anxiety. This kind of cross-sectional research makes it impossible to draw valid inferences about the causal chain of events linking the parental behaviors to the child's anxiety. It is plausible, for instance, that many of the differences observed between such groups of parents are at least as much a *result* of the child's anxiety as they are the cause of the child's anxiety. Another methodological challenge for much of the research in this area relates to the simple fact that parents frequently have more than one child. And so a parent who is being included in the "parents of anxious children" sample may, in fact, also be the parent of one or more not anxious children. While it is common to exclude parents of anxious children from the "healthy control" samples, it is less common to exclude parents from the "parents of anxious children" sample if they also have a healthy, nonanxious, child. These are only some of the challenges facing researchers studying the impact of parental behavior on the development of childhood anxiety. Additional challenges relate to measurement issues, such as the difficulty of accurately and objectively measuring parental behavior (rating scales are inherently subjective; behavior in a laboratory situation may differ from behavior in home), sample sizes, and more.

Even accounting for the many methodological challenges, a synthesis of research in this area suggests that the parental variables account for only a small amount of variation in childhood anxiety outcomes (Bögels & Brechman-Toussaint, 2006). The conclusion must be that either the most influential parental variables have yet to be adequately identified and studied or that parents play a limited role in determining whether a child will or will not experience an anxiety disorder.

Among the parental behaviors that have been most consistently linked to childhood anxiety are behaviors such as overcontrol, low autonomy granting, and overprotection. These closely related constructs refer to a parent's tendency to allow their child to independently explore the world around them, making mistakes along the way and taking some reasonable risks, or to the opposite parental tendency to control a child's behavior, intervene to prevent them from making errors, and take preemptive action to reduce even a low likelihood of them experiencing the slightest harm. Statistically, parents who fall on the more controlling, low-autonomy granting, and protective end of this continuum are more likely to have children with anxiety disorders than those who fall on the opposite end. Yet, as just mentioned, this conclusion should be stated with caution on two counts: First, while statistically significant relations have been found, these have tended to be weak associations such that the child of a controlling, low-autonomy granting, and overprotective parent is only a little more likely to have an anxiety disorder than their peer with very different parents. Second, child anxiety may be statistically linked to this style of parenting without being the outcome of the parenting behaviors. For example, it is plausible that these parental behaviors reflect a genetic predisposition to risk aversion, which is manifesting in one way in the parent and in another in the offspring (although the genetic contribution to the risk of childhood anxiety is modest as well).

As such, identifying *extreme* patterns in parental behaviors that have an outsized likelihood of contributing to a child's well-being is certainly important.

> But suggesting that parents are the cause of their child's anxiety because they show a tendency toward over protectiveness and control is vastly overstating the facts.

Family accommodation, however, is meaningfully different from these parental behaviors and from others such as criticism or rejection, which have also been linked to risk for childhood anxiety. In what way is family accommodation different? Family accommodation is conceptualized as a response to childhood anxiety and must, by definition, follow the onset of a child's anxiety symptoms (although not necessarily an anxiety *disorder*). Parents who are overly protective by trait may also be likely to provide more accommodation of their child's anxiety, and empirical data indicate a small but significant relation between these variables, but the accommodation is not thought of as causing a child to develop anxiety. Simply put, if the child had no anxiety symptoms, there would be nothing for the parent to accommodate, regardless of their parental style and characteristics.

This distinction between parental style and family accommodation is important and is a useful one to convey to parents in beginning to address family accommodation in therapy. Rather than attributing blame by discussing the role of parents in the development of childhood anxiety, the therapist can focus on the natural parental responses to an anxious child.

Indeed, the relation between family accommodation and very desirable parental attributes such as sensitivity to the child, acceptance of the child, and positive regard for the child is stronger than the relation between family accommodation and parental overprotectiveness. Instead of caricaturizing parents as helicopter parents whose child is inevitably anxious due to a lack of autonomy, the therapist can cast the parents in the more generous, and more accurate, role of loving parents who are responding to a child's distress in the most natural way.

Establishing this basis for the discussion of family accommodation makes it easier to continue the discussion of changes in parental behaviors that will further the aim of helping the child to overcome the anxiety. The clinician is likely to find they have forged a more effective therapeutic alliance with the parents of an anxious child if they approach the parents as caring (and often exasperated) caregivers who are doing their best and can benefit from additional expertise and suggestions, rather than as (possibly) well-meaning but inept parents who have stifled their child's autonomy to the point of clinical anxiety.

ACCOMMODATION BY SIBLINGS, TEACHERS, AND OTHERS

Parents are the primary providers of family accommodation but not the exclusive ones. Any person who modifies their behavior to help an anxious child avoid or reduce anxiety can be said to be accommodating, but, of course, those with the most frequent contact with the child and those with the most direct responsibility for the child's functioning are the most important to consider.

Siblings

There is very little research on accommodation of childhood anxiety by siblings (Storch et al., 2007), but clinical experience (and indeed common sense) indicate that siblings, both older and younger, frequently accommodate their anxious sibling. These accommodations can take as many different forms as the accommodations provided by parents but can be usefully divided into three categories, based on the impetus that drives them rather than on the form or function of the accommodation. One category describes accommodations willingly provided by a child, either knowingly or unknowingly, in response to their sibling's anxiety. Siblings will often speak in place of a socially anxious or selectively mute brother or sister, for example. And siblings will commonly accompany a sibling with separation anxiety who avoids being alone. Such accommodations can often be provided unknowingly, meaning that the accommodating child does not perceive the behavior as being a response to anxiety but may see them as merely a request from their brother or sister or may just accept them unquestioningly as how things are. In working with families of anxious children, it is common to encounter children who rely on even very young siblings, oftentimes toddlers, for "accommodation." The younger sibling, of course, does not see the accommodation as such and may even be thrilled by the attention they are receiving from an older, admired sibling.

A second category of accommodations involving siblings describes accommodations by parents that directly or indirectly impact the sibling. These will often engender a sense of resentment in the nonanxious sibling who may feel they are being made to pay an unfair price for their sibling's problems and who, over time, may resist the accommodations. The sibling's feelings of resentment can be further exacerbated if the accommodation is extreme or frequent, or if the parents' motivations are not well explained, or if the sibling rightly or wrongly sees the anxious sibling as taking advantage and as a manipulator of the parent rather than as suffering from the anxiety. Examples of this kind of accommodation range from the benign to situations that border on (or indeed are) maltreatment of the anxious child's sibling. In one example, parents would repeatedly leave movie theaters and restaurants early with both their children, because one child felt anxious about using a public restroom and wanted to return home. In another example, a younger sibling was required to drop a much-loved karate class because her older sister was experiencing panic and agoraphobia and did not feel able to be alone at home while the mother drove to the class. Other examples can include not serving the family foods that one child fears, forbidding a child from touching things their sibling with germ phobia uses, or asking a child not to invite friends over to play because it makes their sibling nervous.

These parent-driven sibling accommodations are a sensitive topic and ought to be broached delicately with parents. A later chapter deals with introducing parents to the topic of accommodation and carefully monitoring accommodation by parents as well as siblings. Here again, however, it is ill-advised to assume that parents are acting out of thoughtlessness or neglect for the well-being of the impacted sibling. When one child in a family is sick, it will often lead to necessary or even critical changes to the behavior of everyone else in the family, including siblings. Family members of children who suffer from severe allergies, diabetes, immunodeficiency illnesses, and many other conditions are generally required to make substantive changes in response to the illness. Parents of an anxious child may see things in similar light and require other children to adapt to the presence of the anxious child.

> *The critical distinction between accommodation of anxiety and of many other illnesses is that family accommodation of child anxiety is neither beneficial to the child nor necessary for recovery.*

Understanding this distinction can be one key to helping parents achieve better balance between what they view as competing needs of their different children. The next chapter discusses this and other motivations that contribute to the high levels of accommodation typically reported by parents of anxious children.

The third category of accommodation provided by siblings are accommodations a sibling provides under duress. It is not rare to see children coerced into accommodating their sibling through fear of physical or psychological aggression. The next chapter deals in some depth with the issue of coercion and family accommodation of childhood anxiety. The chapter focuses primarily on coercion of parents, but siblings too may feel compelled to accommodate a sibling who forcefully demands that they do so. In these cases, it becomes the parents' responsibility, with the help of the therapist, to intervene on behalf of the nonanxious child. Doing so is ultimately beneficial not only to that child but to their anxious (and coercive) sibling as well.

Teachers

The word *accommodation* is often used in the educational setting in a manner that is different from its usage here. In school, accommodations typically refer to individualized adaptations to instruction, requirements, or assessments that are made to support the education of a child with a disability. These accommodations are both necessary and beneficial; however, they are not the topic of this book. Distinguishing between helpful accommodations of this kind and the anxiety accommodations that are discussed here can be challenging. A child may, in fact, benefit from certain accommodations due to an anxiety disorder, and anxiety disorders are legitimate disabilities that must be accommodated in the United States under the Individuals with Disabilities Education Act (IDEA). Yet schools and teachers can also engage in the kind of accommodation that maintains a child's anxiety, rather than improving it, and in those circumstances, accommodation is unhelpful rather than helpful.

One way to distinguish between helpful and unhelpful accommodation is to ask the following question: "Is this accommodation promoting gradually more coping and increased functioning in this child? Or is this accommodation promoting gradually more avoidance and decreased functioning in this child?" When an accommodation is one step on the way from low to high function or from avoiding to not avoiding, it can be helpful. When an accommodation is maintaining avoidance and facilitating increased impairment in an anxious child's functioning, it is unhelpful. It is useful to remember that anxiety, in contrast to some of the conditions covered by IDEA, is a highly treatable condition and that avoidance is a hindrance rather than an aid to recovery. Thus, if a socially anxious child never speaks in class even when called on, and their teacher agrees to not call on them more than once, or to give them a signal prior to calling on them, or even to specifically arrange in advance when they will be called on, these can all be helpful accommodations helping this child to move from complete to partial avoidance. And once the improvement is established, the accommodation can generally be reduced or removed to support even better functioning in the child. Conversely, if a socially anxious child struggles to answer and is visibly uncomfortable when called on in class and a teacher resolves not to call on the child so as to not cause them distress, this is an accommodation that is likely to promote increased avoidance and further impairment. That child may soon feel unable to speak in class at all, even when called on by other teachers.

Communication between the therapist and parents, teachers, and other school personnel is usually key to formulating collaborative treatment plans that allow the child to continue to receive an education, while gradually overcoming their anxiety disorder.

Why Parents Accommodate

Almost all parents of anxious children report engaging in family accommodation of their child's anxiety symptoms. Multiple studies have found that over 95% of mothers of anxious children accommodate their child's anxiety (Lebowitz, Scharfstein, et al., 2014; Lebowitz et al., 2013; Thompson-Hollands et al., 2014). Data on fathers are scarcer, but fathers also report highly prevalent accommodation. So why do so many parents accommodate child anxiety symptoms? Research and clinical work with many families of anxious children suggest a number of prominent factors that contribute to patterns of family accommodation and novel neurobiological research is beginning to reveal the biological infrastructure supporting these patterns.

Of course, every parent is different, and the factors that play the most important roles in driving family accommodation will vary across families. Understanding the motivational profile maintaining family accommodation in a given family, that is, the reasons that a particular parent feels willing or compelled to accommodate, is useful to shaping clinical intervention and developing effective treatment plans for both the parents and the child. This chapter reviews some key reasons that many parents accommodate. Discussing these motivations with parents and considering them while listening to parents describe their accommodating behavior are useful ways to identify key motivational factors for a particular family.

TO REDUCE CHILD DISTRESS

Family accommodation is, by definition, a behavior intended to avoid or reduce a child's distress, and, of course, the natural parental instinct to help a child in distress is central to why parents accommodate. Evolutionary forces have shaped this parental instinct into a powerful force, often strong enough to override other competing considerations. Evolution has likewise equipped children with the ability to signal caregivers when in distress and in need of protection, regulation, or assistance (Harlow, 1960). Starting from the moment of birth, babies respond to needs by signaling their caregivers, "I need you." Whether in need of parents to fend off a threat, to soothe and help restore calm that has been disrupted, or to provide nutrition and nourishment, a young child will instinctively signal the need to a caregiver. Parents are highly sensitive to these child cues, and the urgent need to address them can feel overwhelming. For a parent, seeing a child in a state of fear can feel intolerable and can propel them to act selflessly on the child's behalf.

When parents do not accommodate an anxious child, the result is often a short-term increase in the level of distress the child exhibits. This temporary increase in child anxiety and distress reflects the child's discomfort and frustration but may also be an effective means of getting the parent to accommodate. In many cases, the anguish exhibited by the child has led to accommodating behavior in the past and so has been reinforced by the parent. Reacting to the child's distress by providing accommodation is a form of negative reinforcement that shapes both the child's and the parent's behavior. For the child, the accommodation reduces the anxiety in the near-term and so makes similar displays more likely to recur. For the parent, who observes their child's distress with alarm and consternation, the ability to calm the child likewise provides negative reinforcement for the accommodation and makes the parent more likely to accommodate in the future, even before the child's anxiety reaches extreme levels.

Choosing not to accommodate a child who is feeling scared or anxious is doubly difficult for parents. Not only do they need to contend with the distress their child is feeling, they may also feel guilt at contributing to that distress. A parent who knows that they could reduce their child's suffering by providing accommodation may feel that they are actively hurting their child by choosing not to accommodate. This is not unlike the experience of parents who need to hold a child who is receiving a vaccination or undergoing a painful medical procedure. The parent knows that they are acting for the child's good but also feels deep pain at being the cause of the child's suffering. If a parent is unaware or unconvinced that the accommodation is counterproductive in the long run, or believes that the anxiety and distress are harmful to their child (as discussed next), the challenge can feel insurmountable.

Willful or unintentional manipulation by the anxious child can exacerbate the feelings of guilt in the parent. A distressed child may accuse a parent who does not provide accommodation of not caring about them, not loving them, or even of deliberately wanting to hurt them. Even a parent who knows that the accusations are fueled by the child's distress and frustration and that the child's true feeling of being loved and cared about does not require acquiescence to their desires can find it difficult to persist in not accommodating in the face of these accusations.

BELIEVING THAT ANXIETY IS HARMFUL AND SHOULD BE AVOIDED

This plausible-sounding belief can have pernicious effects on parental behavior. Inevitably, a parent who views anxiety as harmful is going to be motivated to protect their child from experiencing anxiety whenever possible. Ironically, not only is it not true that any experience of anxiety is detrimental to a child's well-being but also striving to avoid the experience of anxiety is virtually tantamount to having an anxiety disorder. Why would this be so? Because most of the impairment associated with anxiety disorders stems from the measures a person takes to avoid feeling anxious. A child or adult who feels anxious in certain situations but accepts this experience as part of life and tolerates the anxiety as a temporary but ultimately benign discomfort is significantly less likely to manifest high levels of impairment, compared to a person who aims to avoid anxiety whenever possible and at great cost. Consider, for example, a child who is tense and anxious before tests but assumes that this is a natural, perhaps an inevitable or even healthy, response to a stressful situation such as taking a test. That child is not likely to become caught up in excessive preparation beyond what is required by the actual test, because they assume the anxiety will be there regardless, and they accept that is how it feels to take tests. They are also not likely to try to avoid school on days when tests occur or to take other maladaptive steps toward avoiding the feeling of anxiety. In contrast, if a child views the same pretest anxiety as intolerable, or even dangerous, they will be motivated to take even extreme measures to avoid it, thereby making it likely that the anxiety-related impairment will grow, leading to further increases in the actual levels of anxiety experienced. Likewise, a parent who views their child's anxiety as dangerous will be motivated to take every possible measure to prevent the anxiety and can further the cycle of anxiety and avoidance.

Many parents report that therapists or other providers have advised them to avoid "triggering" the child and to attempt to keep the environment as stress-free as possible. This advice may be the result of a clinician wrongly conceptualizing the child's problem, or perhaps themselves holding the belief that anxiety is harmful to children, despite empirical evidence to the contrary. In most cases, such advice serves to reinforce the parental notion that anxiety is harmful to the child and to strengthen the parents' belief that their role is to remove anxiety from the child's life whenever possible. Research indicates that coping with moderate levels of anxiety in the context of healthy and supportive adult relationships actually increases children's coping skills and promotes resilience. Every child and parent will require a unique treatment plan suited to their particular circumstances and situation, but a plan that centers around eliminating anxiety altogether is neither feasible nor desirable.

THE NEED FOR SHORT-TERM CHILD OR FAMILY FUNCTIONING

Very often the choice faced by parents is not merely a choice between accommodating or not accommodating. It can also be a choice between accommodating and significant disruption to the functioning of the anxious child or even the entire family. Consider a parent putting an anxious child to bed alongside one or more siblings. The anxious child may request that the parent stay with them until they fall asleep. The parent may also know from experience that if not accommodated, the anxious child will cry loudly for a long time, keeping their siblings awake and making it difficult for the parent to accomplish anything else until calm is restored. The choice whether or not to accommodate is inextricably intertwined with the need to consider the effects on the other family members. The next morning the same parent may be attempting to leave the house, get all the children to school, and arrive to work on time, when the anxious child refuses to leave the house unless the parent promises to be home at a certain time, or unless the parent accompanies them to their room to retrieve a book because they are fearful of going alone, or unless the parent reviews their homework one more time. Each of these would once again pit any inclination not to accommodate the anxiety against the needs of the rest of the family, and of the anxious child themselves, as they too have to arrive at school (preferably in a state of calm).

Understanding the pressures faced by parents, through the ongoing need to maintain family functioning for the entire family, is crucial both to empathizing with the dilemma in which the parents are caught and to shaping feasible treatment plans that will be put into practice. A plan, no matter how elegantly crafted by a skilled clinician, is unlikely to survive the stresses of reality if these are unfamiliar to the clinician or not considered in the plan's formulation.

TO PROTECT THE CHILD'S SOCIAL STATUS

Parents may also worry that not accommodating the child's anxiety will lead to negative impact on the child's social status or cause them to be judged negatively by peers or others. The most common, though by no means only, example of this is the parent who speaks on behalf of a child to mask the child's social anxiety or avoid it being overly obtrusive. Additional examples include accommodations that enable a child to attend social gatherings and school events, because a parent is concerned that without the accommodation the child will not go at all, or a parent who engages in accommodations to prevent a child from becoming distraught and causing a scene in front of peers. In some cases, this may be a valid concern, with true potential for negative social impact should the parent not accommodate. In other cases, the parents' fear may be unwarranted and may reflect their own social evaluative concerns. Either way, while not usually a good rationale for maintaining the accommodation over time, this motivation too needs to be addressed by the therapist if they are too offer advice that parents can put into practice outside of the therapy office.

PARENT ANXIETY

Genetic and nongenetic heritability, as well as the overall high prevalence of anxiety disorders in the population, make it certain that many of the anxious children seen in practice will have at least one anxious parent as well (Eley et al.,

2015; Lebowitz, Leckman, Silverman, & Feldman, 2016). A parent's anxiety can contribute to family accommodation in several ways. An anxious parent may identify strongly with their anxious child and the distress the child is feeling and may be even more powerfully motivated to "rescue" their child from this distress or to provide them with a sense of security they themselves have felt lacking. Anxious parents may also be more likely to believe that anxiety can be harmful, having suffered from anxiety in their own lives, and thus be more inclined to accommodate their child. A parent who has a strong predisposition to anxiety may have developed an avoidant coping style and may see accommodation as the most natural and accessible response to a stressful situation. Or, an anxious parent may not be well equipped with alternative coping strategies and skills and may struggle to find other, nonaccommodating responses to the situation.

Parental anxiety can contribute to a parent's accommodating but does not preclude the parent learning and implementing alternatives offered and taught by a sensitive and well-informed clinician. Many anxious parents respond with relief to alternatives when they are offered, often remarking that they "wish someone had taught their own parents to act this way." Assessing parental anxiety in working with anxious children is useful and provides valuable information. But the presence of elevated parental anxiety need not be an impediment to work with the child or the parent, nor is it equivalent to an understanding of the causes of the child's anxiety.

AGGRESSIVE CHILD BEHAVIOR

Alongside the more tender feelings that motivate much of the accommodation provided by parents, the goal of avoiding unpleasant or destructive child behaviors is a powerful force driving family accommodation. Anxious children are themselves powerfully motivated to obtain the accommodation and will frequently employ all possible means in furthering this aim. Angry outbursts, rage, verbal aggression, and even physical violence toward person or property are not uncommon in children when parents do not provide accommodation. Several studies have indicated that maintaining family accommodation is a common function of aggressive behaviors in children with anxiety disorders or obsessive-compulsive disorder (Johnco et al., 2015; Lebowitz, Panza, et al., 2016; McGuire et al., 2013). Parents are more likely to accommodate when the accommodation helps to avoid or reduce aggressive behavior in the child. As noted earlier, another form of coercion frequently displayed by anxious children seeking to maintain parental accommodation is the use of emotionally laden accusations directed at the parents ("emotional blackmail"). Children may accuse parents of not loving or caring about them, caring more about another child or themselves, not wanting to help them and so forth. A parent faced with this kind of accusation may feel that providing the accommodation is the only way to demonstrate their care for the child or convince them that they are loved.

Even children who are generally not otherwise prone to externalizing symptoms can use aggression to elicit accommodation from their parents. In these children, the aggression may be even more impactful on parents, who may be stunned by seeing such behaviors in their child. For this reason, even in cases of children who have not exhibited problematic behaviors in the past, clinicians working with anxious children and their parents should prepare the parents for the possibility of child aggression prior to initiating changes to parental accommodating behavior. Parents who are not prepared emotionally for the possibility of child aggression and who are not equipped to respond to it in a deliberate manner are likely to either retreat from their plan and resume the accommodation or escalate the conflict through impulsive and unhelpful responses.

The high rates of co-morbidity between anxiety disorders and externalizing disorders such as oppositional defiant disorder or attention deficit/hyperactivity disorder mean that inevitably some anxious children will also have a history of aggressive or destructive behaviors that is not related directly to the anxiety disorder (Costello, Egger, Copeland, Erkanli, & Angold, 2011). Irritability is also common in anxious children (Poznanski et al., 2017; Stoddard et al., 2014) and is often a developmental antecedent of anxiety in young children. Parents of children who have a history of aggressive behaviors may be less taken aback by their child becoming aggressive when requesting accommodation but may also be weary of the behavioral problems and inclined to provide the accommodation to avoid additional confrontations with their child.

Finally, an additional form of aggression sometimes used by children to induce parents to accommodate is the use of threats directed toward the child's self. Suicidal statements or gestures, whether calculated or in the heat of the moment, are not uncommon and can override even the strongest parent's resolve. While generally not reflecting a grave risk of actual self-harm, such statements or gestures should not be taken lightly. A later chapter describes tools for coping with children's aggressive, destructive, and self-threatening responses to not being accommodated.

Theoretical Basis and Mechanisms of Action

3

Why Accommodation Matters

Negative Impact of Parent Accommodation

The previous chapter described many of the motivating forces driving family accommodation of childhood anxiety. Underpinning all these motivations is the parents' desire to reduce anxiety in their child. The thing that makes accommodation into a veritable trap, with the potential to ensnare parents and children in an inextricable and endless spiral of anxiety and accommodation, is that accommodation actually leads to more, rather than less, anxiety symptoms. This is the essence of the "accommodation trap": Parents accommodate to reduce child anxiety, but more accommodation predicts more severe child anxiety, usually leading to even more accommodation (Figure 3.1).

Numerous studies have documented the link between greater levels of family accommodation and worse child anxiety (Kagan, Peterman, Carper, & Kendall, 2016; Lebowitz, Panza, et al., 2016; Lebowitz et al., 2013; Norman, Silverman, & Lebowitz, 2015; Reuman & Abramowitz, 2017; Storch et al., 2015). It is likely that higher levels of accommodation reflect, at least in part, the severity of the child's symptoms. That is to say, if a child is more anxious, there may be more symptoms for parents to accommodate, and ratings of accommodation are likely to be higher. But the data also suggest the inverse relation. That when a child is accommodated to a higher degree, the result is more anxiety symptoms over time. Furthermore, highly accommodated children also experience more anxiety-related impairment in multiple domains of their daily functioning and are less likely to benefit from front-line treatments such as cognitive-behavioral therapy and medication.

The relation between symptom severity and higher levels of accommodation was described first in studies of childhood obsessive-compulsive disorder (OCD) and replicated in several childhood anxiety studies. The very first investigation of family accommodation in pediatric anxiety disorders, published in 2013, already reported highly significant correlations between family accommodation and child anxiety symptom severity (Lebowitz et al., 2013). The degree of family accommodation reported by parents explained over 20% of variance in child anxiety symptom severity. Subsequent studies have confirmed this link and demonstrated that the association holds even across informants (Lebowitz et al., 2015). Child

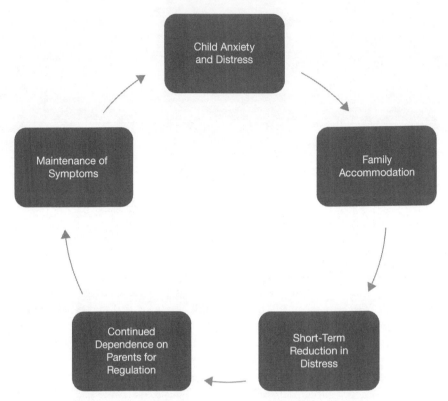

Figure 3.1 Family accommodation reduces child anxiety in the short-term but can maintain the child's dependence on parents and lead to more anxiety symptoms over time.

ratings of their parents' accommodation are correlated with parental ratings of child anxiety, and parent-rated family accommodation correlates with children's ratings of their own anxiety symptoms. This kind of cross-informant validation strengthens the confidence in the validity of the correlation being described between family accommodation and the severity of child anxiety symptoms.

Family accommodation is associated not only with the severity of anxiety symptoms but also with anxiety-related impairment, or the degree of interference that the anxiety symptoms cause in the child's daily life (Stewart et al., 2011; Thompson-Hollands et al., 2014). Impairment is assessed in the most important domains of a child's functioning: school attendance and performance, social functioning and peer relations, and home life including getting along with parents and siblings and being able to maintain daily routines such as sleeping and eating. Anxious children whose families accommodate more to their symptoms are likely to experience correspondingly higher levels of interference in each of these important domains.

Research has also indicated that high levels of family accommodation may interfere with a child's ability to benefit from treatment for their anxiety. The first study to provide compelling evidence for the relation between high levels of family accommodation and poor treatment outcomes in children focused on accommodation of childhood OCD (Garcia et al., 2010). An analysis of outcomes from the Pediatric Obsessive-Compulsive Treatment Study (POTS), the largest randomized controlled trial of childhood OCD, sought to identify predictors and moderators of outcomes in participating subjects. The study looked at numerous variables, including child, parent, and family characteristics. Of all the hypothesized family characteristics that were considered, only family accommodation was found to significantly predict treatment response. What was particularly striking in the study results was that family accommodation predicted poor treatment response regardless of the kind of treatment the child received. Children in POTS were randomly assigned to receive either cognitive-behavioral therapy, medication (sertraline, a selective serotonin reuptake inhibitor [SSRI]), or a combination of both therapies. Across all three treatment conditions, children fared worse and had more severe symptoms at the end of the clinical trial when they were more heavily accommodated at home.

The degree to which family accommodation predicts treatment outcomes for childhood anxiety disorders has not yet been well established. Preliminary indications, however, are that, as in OCD, higher levels of family accommodation predict poor treatment response. One study, for example, examined treatment response in anxious children who received cognitive-behavioral therapy (Salloum et al., 2018). Children whose parents endorsed more accommodating responses to hypothetical vignettes describing situations with their anxious child responded worse to treatment and had more severe anxiety symptoms at the end of the clinical trial, compared with children whose parents endorsed less accommodating responses. Currently, ongoing research is examining this question in larger clinical trials using the ratings of actual accommodation provided by both children and parents.

In addition to the impact of family accommodation on the child's symptoms, impairment, and treatment response, it is also important to consider the impact of accommodation on the other members of the anxious child's family. Parents consistently report that providing accommodation for their anxious child causes them high levels of distress and interferes with the family's ability to function normally. This is not surprising, as parents often invest tremendous time and energy in accommodating their anxious child. The time diverted away from other activities and responsibilities, the frequent intrusions to personal space, the infringement on workplace productivity or schedule, and the frustration and helplessness that come from seeing the child's anxiety grow worse despite all these sacrifices contribute to the harrowing burden experienced by parents of anxious children.

The "accommodation trap" described in relation to the child's symptom severity, holds true for child and family functioning as well. Parents accommodate, often to enable the child or family to achieve functional goals such as getting to sleep or to school, but the accommodation actually leads to greater functional impairment at both the individual and family levels. To successfully modify parental behavior and reduce accommodation, the therapist will need to consider the impact on these near-term goals and prepare parents for alternative coping strategies and for the possibility that things may actually be harder in the short-term.

Family accommodation can also take a toll on the parents' relationship with the anxious child. Parents frequently become resentful and irate about the demands placed on them by the child's anxiety and can express this resentment in various ways. From the perspective of the child, the need for accommodation will generally overpower their dismay about their parents' discontent but can leave them feeling ashamed or inadequate. Ratings provided by children consistently indicate that they are aware that the need to accommodate them is distressing to their parents, and they even acknowledge that accommodation is not helpful in reducing their anxiety over the long-term. But children also report that they prefer their parents continue to accommodate them, nonetheless.

A previous chapter discussed accommodation provided by siblings, as well as parents, and the involvement of siblings in accommodating an anxious child adds another layer of disruption to family functioning. The examples of the sibling who is forced to drop a karate class because another sibling is too anxious about being home alone or who has to interrupt a movie because it is making their sibling anxious illustrate the toll that sibling accommodation can take on the entire family. Siblings may feel resentful about the attention that the anxious is child is receiving "at their expense" or about impositions placed on them out of consideration for another child's anxiety. And siblings may be more likely than parents to voice their disgruntlement, contributing to intrafamily conflict and hostility. Even when not directly involved, siblings may feel impinged upon by their brother or sister's anxiety and by the displays of anger or distress that motivate their parents to accommodate.

WHY DOES ACCOMMODATION HAVE SUCH NEGATIVE IMPACT?

Accommodation Promotes Avoidance

Avoidance is the natural response to fear and anxiety. By avoiding feared situations, anxiety is maintained over time and tends to be chronic, rarely remitting spontaneously. Avoidance is also generalized, gradually increasing in scope. This "avoidance creep" contributes to the gradual exacerbation in anxiety symptoms that characterizes the clinical course of anxiety disorders. Consistent avoidance limits the natural opportunities for desensitization and prevents new learning or the modification of negative expectations necessary for recovery from anxiety disorders.

Family accommodation makes it easier for a child to avoid anxiety-provoking situations and facilitates avoidance. By taking on responsibilities that would otherwise fall to the child, participating in anxious symptoms and modifying family routines to prevent the child from experiencing anxiety, parents can help a child to avoid confronting their fears.

Eliana began to exhibit school refusal behavior in the third grade. She would wake up in the morning feeling sick to her stomach and beg to stay home. On some days Eliana would refuse to leave the house and her parents, Myles and Sarah, would have to drag her physically to get her in to the car. Each year Eliana missed more and more days of school. She told her parents that school did not feel safe. She thought other children did not like her and that her teachers were against her. Any harsh word from a peer or a teacher would stick in her memory, while friendly overtures and positive feedback never seemed to make any difference at all. Finally, in the sixth grade her parents decided to homeschool her. They were exhausted from the constant struggle and felt it was unfair to Eliana to make her attend a school that felt unsafe. They discussed switching schools, but Eliana was confident things would be the same anywhere and told them that she would refuse to speak at any meeting with a new school. They convened a meeting at school together with Eliana's therapist, who advocated for the home schooling, citing Eliana's generalized anxiety disorder and social phobia as disabilities that prevented her from attending school. The school psychologist was wary of further deterioration in Eliana's anxiety if she was to be kept at home, but most of the school team was feeling frustrated with Eliana's chronic absences and complaints, and the school agreed to provide a home tutor. The school psychologist recommended the tutoring occur outside of the home, at the library or even in school after hours, but after two attempts at getting Eliana to arrive at out-of-home tutoring sessions the lessons were relocated to the home.

Eliana's case is typical of anxious children who have persistent difficulty in attending school. Gradually increasing school refusal behavior often leads to a complete abandonment of functional expectations outside of the home and to heavy accommodation that maintains a child's avoidance over lengthy periods of time. Eliana's caregivers faced a challenging situation. Valiant efforts to maintain attendance seemed to have failed, and therapy had not been successful in reducing her negative reactions to school. The result, however, is a retreat from normative and age-appropriate functional expectations, facilitated by a collaborative accommodation of her anxiety. The parents are accommodating Eliana's anxiety by allowing her to stay home and avoid the discomfort of school, the therapist is contributing to the accommodation through the recommendation that Eliana be homeschooled, and the professional opinion that she is not able to attend school, and the school is facilitating the accommodation by providing the home tutoring. The tutor, too, though not responsible for Eliana's socioemotional development, is enabling further increased accommodation by conducting the sessions at home, rather than outside as recommended in the educational plan. In Eliana's case, only the school psychologist is explicitly voicing the concern that providing this kind of extensive accommodation may lead to increased rather than reduced anxiety. But the school psychologist is unable to return the child to school and is overruled by the other team members.

Family accommodation enables avoidance of both external objects and situations and of internal experiences of anxiety and distress. When parents open a door for a child with OCD or a germ phobia, or avoid outings to crowded places, or rush to take a child home so they avoid using a public restroom, they are helping the child to avoid confronting a situation that triggers anxiety. When parents answer repeated reassurance seeking questions for a child with generalized anxiety or participate in the confession rituals of a child with OCD, for example, they are helping the child to avoid internal experiences of anxiety. In both cases, the family accommodation promotes avoidance, helping to explain the links between family accommodation and the severity of anxious children's symptoms, as well as their poorer prognostic profile.

Accommodation Reduces Self-Regulation

A previous chapter described the natural tendency of babies and young children to rely on attachment figures for protection and regulation and the natural parental drive to provide these important functions. As children grow older, the dependence on attachment figures is gradually reduced, as children develop greater ability to defend themselves, and to regulate their own internal states. This developmental shift is observed both behaviorally, in the shift toward more independent responses to anxiety, and neurologically. Brain imaging studies have shown a shift away from reliance on parental presence, toward more independent regulation of activity in areas of the brain implicated in the anxiety response, as children get older (Gee et al., 2014). Anxious children face a more difficult challenge in accomplishing this developmental transition, because they experience anxiety more frequently and acutely and because of differences in the biological systems that enable self-regulation.

Family accommodation may further compound the difficulty in the development of self-regulatory skills, by reducing opportunities to practice self-regulation and by continually reinforcing the less mature, parent-dependent regulatory system. An anxious child who seeks reassurance from a parent because they are feeling worried is less likely to practice independent coping strategies such as reassessment of pertinent information, distraction, physical regulation through relaxation or exercise, or nonparental social supports. The child's independent skills remain less well developed, further promoting reliance on family accommodation, in an ongoing cycle of anxiety and accommodation.

Many parents are surprised when they begin to reduce their family accommodation to discover that their child is actually capable of more self-regulation than they thought possible. By stepping in to provide accommodation, they have been reinforcing their belief that this is the only manner in which their child is able to feel better. This belief is frequently shared by their child as well, as discussed next.

Accommodation Reduces a Child's Confidence in Themselves

Parents are not the only ones who can underestimate a child's ability for independent coping with anxiety. Very often children misjudge their own ability as well. Cognitive-behavioral therapists who encourage anxious children to practice exposures to feared situations typically ask the child to rate the degree of discomfort they expect a given exposure will cause and then to rate the actual discomfort they experienced during the exposure. It is common for the actual ratings to be significantly lower than the predicted rating (though the opposite occurs as well). This happens both because of the catastrophizing characteristic of anxious children thoughts and because having avoided exposure for a long time, the child underestimates their ability to handle the situation. In much the same manner, children who are accommodated by their parents strengthen their belief that they are not capable of handling their anxiety alone.

Parents are the mirror that children look into to see themselves. This applies broadly to children's self-image but is particularly relevant for anxious children's belief in their capacity for self-regulation. If parental reactions and responses reflect to the child an image of themselves as helpless and defenseless in the face of anxiety, it is likely that the child will see themselves this way. By accommodating an anxious child, parents may be telling the child "I know you can't cope with anxiety, so I'm going to help you." The anxiety may be reduced in the near-term, but a child who continually interprets their parents' behavior in this manner will feel less confident and more vulnerable over time, again leading to a cycle of anxiety and accommodation.

Accommodation Reduces Insight

Anxiety leads to cognitive distortions, such as the exaggerated estimation of risks and the misinterpretation of realistically neutral cues as danger signals. Alongside the behavioral work of exposure, cognitive-behavioral therapy emphasizes cognitive restructuring, or the identification and correction of these cognitive distortions. By providing family accommodation, parents may inadvertently hamper a child's ability to correctly label anxious thoughts as unrealistic or exaggerated (Adelman & Lebowitz, 2012).

> *Muhammad was constantly worried about burglars and kidnappers. Muhammad refused to stay home alone and each night would ask his parents repeatedly if they thought the home would be broken into. One night his parents woke up to find Muhammad in their room trembling. Muhammad had heard a sound and thought an intruder was in the house. The next morning his father said "That's it, we're putting in an alarm system." He took Muhammad with him to shop for the new alarm and asked the salesman to explain to Muhammad how hard it would be for anyone to break in undetected. The*

*salesman impressed Muhammad with details about the various kinds of
sensors employed by the top-notch system, and the short response time whenever an alarm is triggered. Once the alarm was installed, Muhammad's father
called him over to watch him activating it at night, telling his wife "Maybe this
way he'll let us sleep at night!"*

Muhammad's father is attempting to reduce his son's anxiety (and to get some
sleep) by accommodating the fear of burglars. From Muhammad's perspective,
however, his father's actions may actually confirm that his concerns are valid.
After all, if dad is spending this much money on an alarm, there must be a good
chance of burglars breaking in.

Even when parents verbally assure a child that their fears are unwarranted or
their anxiety is irrational, their accommodating behavior can deliver the opposite
message to the child. An anxious child is more likely to focus on what their parent
is actually doing than on what they are saying. A child with separation anxiety who
believes she cannot stay home alone may be told many times that there is nothing to
worry about, but if her parents always stay with her, their actions suggest otherwise.
The parents may believe they are staying with the child only because of her anxiety
and not because of any realistic threat to her safety, but there is no guarantee that
their daughter will perceive their actions in this manner. Similarly, parents may tell
a socially anxious child that there is no reason to fear being ridiculed, but keeping
her out of social events may convey the opposite message. Or the parents of a child
with contamination fears may explain again and again that the fears are not genuine health concerns, but if they continue to buy excessive amounts of soap, the
child may take their actions as confirmation of the anxious beliefs about germs. And
parents of a child who fears being seriously ill or interprets the symptoms of anxiety
as signs of disease may be suggesting that they share these concerns by taking the
child to medical examinations, even when they themselves believe the child to be
in good physical health. And so rather than reducing anxiety, accommodation can
contribute to lower insight in the child and to more severe symptoms over time.

Even skilled therapists can fall into the trap of providing accommodation, in the
guise of cognitive restructuring. A child with a persistent irrational thought can
engage a therapist in endless cognitive restructuring exercises, with the therapist
time and again examining the facts, leading Socratic dialogues, and challenging
the distorted cognition. When this occurs, it is useful to consider the possibility
that, rather than confronting their faulty cognition, the child is actually seeking
repeated reassurance from the therapist. If true, the cognitive work has actually
become a form of accommodation and is unlikely to help advance the therapeutic
process if continued unabated.

Accommodation Reduces Motivation for Treatment

Not all children with anxiety disorders, even severe ones, are motivated to confront their fears or engage in therapy. Estimating the number of treatment-refusing

children with anxiety disorders is difficult as many children will refuse even to participate in assessment or evaluation. Even among children who do present for evaluation and who are offered treatment, however, the number of children who decline to participate is high. And even when a child is participating in therapy, motivation remains an issue. Anxiety treatment is hard, and successful therapy usually relies on practice and implementation between therapy sessions. Exposures in particular are difficult as the child is being asked to face things that trigger intense fear and that have long been avoided. Motivation is key to overcoming these difficulties, and a child who lacks sufficient motivation may not be able to benefit from the therapy.

The need to confront anxiety in various situations can help motivate a child to overcome their fears. Family accommodation provides the child with an alternative strategy, which, while not leading to less anxiety over time, enables them to escape feeling anxious in the short-term and can contribute to diminished motivation for treatment. When a child with panic and agoraphobia, for example, is allowed to leave school when they feel panicky, or a child with social phobia is permitted to avoid the school lunchroom and to eat in a teacher's lounge, or a child with separation anxiety sleeps in their parents' bed, they may feel less motivated to engage in a therapeutic process aimed at helping them to cope with these situations. Even when a child would like, in principle, to be able to feel less afraid and acknowledges that their fear is having a negative impact on their lives, accommodation can reduce motivation for treatment. Faced with the choice between working hard and facing their fears or continuing to rely on accommodations, many children will understandably choose the latter. By reducing the accommodation, parents can help the child to feel that overcoming the anxiety is imperative, making them more likely to engage in, and to benefit from, treatment.

4

Reducing Accommodation to Treat Child Anxiety

The intense focus on family accommodation research in recent years, establishing its importance in the maintenance and clinical course of childhood anxiety disorders, has also sparked considerable interest in the reduction of family accommodation as a therapeutic intervention. Researchers and clinicians are asking the questions: Will reducing family accommodation also reduce childhood anxiety? Will it improve treatment outcomes in standard treatment modalities? And if accommodation reduction is a useful tool in treating childhood anxiety, should it be done alongside other therapies? In place of them? Or perhaps before, or after, delivery of treatments such cognitive-behavioral therapy or medications? The answers to some of these questions are gradually being established. For others, there remains a dearth of empirical data on which to base recommendations, and clinicians continue to rely on their clinical judgement, patient preferences, and trial and error in shaping treatment plans. The current chapter addresses these questions and introduces some useful points to contemplate in considering when and how to focus on accommodation reduction in the treatment of childhood anxiety.

REDUCING ACCOMMODATION AS A STAND-ALONE TREATMENT

By far, the bulk of research on parent-based interventions for childhood anxiety has investigated parent work as an added component, alongside child therapy, rather than as an independent stand-alone therapeutic protocol (Barmish & Kendall, 2005; Breinholst, Esbjorn, Reinholdt-Dunne, & Stallard, 2012; Manassis et al., 2014; Nauta, Scholing, Emmelkamp, & Minderaa, 2001). Furthermore, studies of parent-based treatment have generally not focused on the reduction of accommodation as the primary treatment objective of the parent work. Rather, the emphasis has mostly been on reinforcing the cognitive-behavioral skills taught in the child's therapy by teaching them to parents as well as the child. These treatment protocols generally include at least some guidance encouraging parents to refrain from facilitating child avoidance but do not make the assessment and systematic reduction of family accommodation a central treatment goal and do not include tools for coping with the difficult reactions observed in many children when parents decrease accommodation. The secondary role of accommodation reduction and the absence of pragmatic strategies for overcoming difficult child reactions decrease the likelihood that parents will significantly reduce the accommodation they provide.

An exception to this description of parent work in childhood anxiety is a parent-based treatment that has been delivered as a stand-alone therapy without concurrent childhood treatment and that focuses on accommodation reduction as a primary treatment objective. The Supportive Parenting for Anxious Childhood Emotions (SPACE) Program was developed with these objectives and has been empirically tested in two pilot clinical trials and a randomized controlled trial (Lebowitz, 2013; Lebowitz, Omer, Hermes, & Scahill, 2014; Lebowitz et al. 2019). The initial open trials of SPACE focused on children who either refused to participate in cognitive-behavioral therapy or had received cognitive-behavioral therapy but had failed to improve significantly following therapy. Focusing on this population of anxious children helps to establish the usefulness of SPACE as an alternative treatment strategy in cases where direct child therapy is not feasible or effective. Children in both pilot studies had significantly reduced anxiety symptoms following the parent-based treatment. Parents expressed high satisfaction with the treatment, further supporting the feasibility of treating childhood anxiety in this manner.

Following the open trials, a randomized controlled trial was undertaken. One hundred and twenty children were randomly assigned to receive 12 weeks of either cognitive-behavioral therapy or SPACE. In each case, only one treatment was provided, allowing for comparisons in outcomes between the two therapies and for examination of possible moderators of treatment outcome. Results from the randomized trial confirm that SPACE reduces childhood anxiety symptoms. What is particularly striking in the results of the randomized trial is that children in both conditions showed similar, and not statistically different, degrees of improvement. Also notable, children and parents both endorsed significant posttreatment improvement, regardless of treatment condition, as did independent evaluators who were uninformed of the treatment condition. Children and parents also expressed similar levels of satisfaction with both treatments.

It is thus possible to treat anxiety by reducing parental accommodation even in the absence of direct child therapy. In many cases, however, the most sensible course of action may be to work with both child and parents, providing cognitive-behavioral therapy as well as reducing family accommodation, as discussed next.

REDUCING ACCOMMODATION AS PART OF A LARGER TREATMENT STRATEGY

A comprehensive treatment strategy for childhood anxiety may include both child therapy, potentially including medication as well as cognitive-behavioral therapy, and parent work to reduce family accommodation. Studies that have compared child-only therapy to child therapy augmented by parent work have so far not provided convincing evidence that the combined child and parent approach leads to better outcomes. However, as described in the previous section, the parent work has mostly focused on augmenting the cognitive-behavioral therapy by teaching parents cognitive-behavioral strategies and has not focused on reducing accommodation. These studies have also been relatively small in sample sizes and have yielded very limited information about possible moderators of treatment response. Moderators of treatment response are variables that predict differential response to various treatment modalities. In other words, rather than addressing the question, "Which treatment approach is better overall?" moderators answer the question, "Which treatment approach is better for which patients?" An examination of moderators in a large clinical trial for child anxiety, Childhood Anxiety Multimodal Study (CAMS), for example, indicated that for children with severe anxiety disorders, cognitive-behavioral therapy alone is insufficient (Taylor et al., 2018). CAMS randomized close to 500 children to receive either cognitive-behavioral therapy, medication (sertraline) or the combination of both cognitive-behavioral therapy and medication. A fourth group received only a placebo medication. While all three treatment groups showed significant improvement, with the combined treatment group showing only modest benefit relative to the two stand-alone treatments, this pattern did not hold true for the children who entered the study with high anxiety severity. In this high severity group, only children who received the combined treatment approach showed improvement that was statistically significantly better than children in the placebo group. Even though studies have yet to demonstrate significant enhancement of treatment outcomes when parent work is added to cognitive-behavioral therapy, it is plausible that a stronger focus on reducing accommodation would show greater enhancement of the parent work and that certain groups of patients, such as those with severe anxiety, would show enhanced outcomes even if the overall sample did not.

A number of studies in childhood obsessive-compulsive disorder (OCD) have reported better outcomes when working with parents alongside cognitive-behavioral therapy with the child, though here too the emphasis on reducing family accommodation has been quite limited. In some of these studies, the parent component has focused on teaching parents behavior management techniques. In another, recent study the researchers focused on children with OCD whose families had high levels of blame, conflict, or other indicators of poor family functioning (Peris, Rozenman, Sugar, McCracken, & Piacentini, 2017). Participants received either cognitive-behavioral therapy or cognitive-behavioral therapy augmented with a family-based component that included, among other things, training parents on disengagement from family accommodation. In this sample of children from poorly functioning households characterized by low cohesion and high conflict and blame, children who received the combined child and family therapy showed significantly better treatment response, compared to those who received just cognitive-behavioral therapy.

No studies have yet examined enhancement to cognitive- behavioral therapy through parent work focused mainly or exclusively on reducing accommodation, but these examples suggest such an approach is feasible and likely to be effective.

As previously noted, high levels of family accommodation predict poor response to cognitive-behavioral therapy for child anxiety and OCD (Garcia et al., 2010). One way in which family accommodation may interfere with child therapy is by making it harder or less likely for a child to practice exposures outside of the therapy session. For example, if a child with social phobia is assigned the out-of-office exposure of speaking for themselves in a public setting, then a parent who accommodates by speaking in place of the child may make it less likely for the exposure to occur. Combining parent work to help parents identify their accommodations and reduce them may help the child to benefit more from their own therapy, as well as reducing the child's anxiety directly.

Sequencing

A remaining question relates to the optimal sequencing of parent and child treatment when integrating accommodation reduction alongside cognitive-behavioral therapy with the child. It may be useful in many cases to precede the child treatment with some parent-focused sessions to begin the process of accommodation reduction and potentially increase the child's motivation for therapy. On the other hand, it may be easier for some parents to reduce accommodation after they begin to see some improvement in their child's anxiety or know that their child is being equipped with tools to handle the anxiety provoking accommodation reduction. It may also be that beginning both treatment components together is the optimal strategy for some families, with each component enhancing and promoting the other and with a degree of coordination between the focus of the parental changes and the targets of the child work. In the absence of empirical data to guide decision-making, clinicians will rely on their judgement and on family preferences, both parent's and child's. However, a number of considerations may help to inform the decision to focus on one or the other treatment modality, and their relative sequencing, which are discussed next.

DEVELOPING A TREATMENT PLAN THAT INCLUDES ACCOMMODATION REDUCTION

Child Age

Some studies have reported an inverse relation between the anxious child's age and the degree of reported family accommodation, such that younger children were accommodated more than older ones. While not a consistent result, it may be that as parents are inherently more involved in the lives of younger children, their degree of enmeshment in the child's anxiety symptoms is also greater. Parents tend to spend more time with younger children, are more involved in their regular functioning such as eating and sleeping, and may also be more willing to accommodate a younger child than an older one. Older children may also be more able to decline to participate in therapy themselves, as it becomes harder for parents to impose decisions about activities in their child's lives. It may be useful to consider introducing the parent work earlier with younger patients, in light of these considerations. One contrary argument, however, is that if, indeed, parents usually accommodate older children less, then a teenager or adolescent presenting with high degrees of accommodation may be in particular need of parent work to target the accommodation.

Child Motivation

If a child presents with little or no motivation for therapy, the likelihood of a successful intervention with the child is markedly reduced. Treatment motivation and expectancies (the degree to which a patient believes a therapy will help) have been found to predict outcomes and treatment response (Chu & Kendall, 2004). In cases of low motivation, an effort can be made to increase the child's motivation, through motivational interviewing or other techniques. However, low motivation can also be associated with high degrees of family accommodation. Ascertaining the amount of accommodation provided and probing the relation between accommodation and the child's motivation is sensible. Working with the parents of such a child sooner rather than later can be a useful strategy. Reducing the degree of family accommodation may help to increase the child's motivation by making avoidance more difficult to maintain. And if motivation remains low and the child does not engage in productive therapy themselves, the parent work presents an alternative treatment strategy that does not rely on the child's collaboration. Parents of children who refuse therapy often feel helpless, unable to provide what they know is likely to be helpful to a child who is suffering. Providing effective parent-based treatment empowers parents by offering them an alternative means of helping their child, relieving the sense of helplessness and frustration.

Child's Ability to Engage in Therapy

Other factors, apart from motivation, can also impede direct child-based therapy. Cognitive limitations, attentional problems, language barriers, and social and communicative deficits can hinder therapeutic efforts. Children with serious behavioral problems may also be challenging patients who are difficult to work with directly. Other co-morbid conditions such as depression can likewise reduce the likelihood of successful child therapy. In these or other situations in which a child's ability to engage in therapy is constrained, parent work to reduce the degree of family accommodation will be particularly indicated.

Degree of Family Accommodation

A final consideration is the degree of family accommodation currently provided to the child. Though almost all anxious children are accommodated by
their parents to some degree, there is a broad range and considerable variance among families. Assessment and case formulation for childhood anxiety
disorders should always include a focus on family accommodation, and higher
levels of accommodation can indicate more pressing need for parent work.
In addition to the degree of family accommodation, the more specific forms
and content of accommodations being provided can help inform the decision
to work with parents. For example, a child who is being accommodated by
allowing them to avoid important functions such as school may require more
urgent parent-based intervention than one whose accommodations have less
immediately detrimental impact. And accommodations that are harmful to
other family members, or that cause considerable strife in the family, or that
are humiliating or abhorrent to someone in the family will indicate the need
to introduce parent work more swiftly than accommodations that are more benign in their impact.

ADDITIONAL BENEFITS OF REDUCING
FAMILY ACCOMMODATION

The primary goals of reducing family accommodation are to improve child anxiety and, in some cases, to facilitate additional treatment modalities. However,
successfully reducing family accommodation can have additional benefits that are
also worthy of consideration and that correspond to the detrimental influences of
accommodation described in a previous chapter.

Improved Family Functioning

Family accommodation of an anxious child can have a negative, and sometimes dev-
astating, impact on the entire family. Reducing family accommodation can significantly improve family functioning in multiple domains. When the accommodation
leads to a fraught, tense, or hostile environment, decreasing the accommodation
will often also reduce the level of tension and improve the household atmosphere.
Parental conflict can be exacerbated by accommodation, as parents argue about how
best to respond to the anxious child or criticize each other for what they perceive
as unhelpful or even harmful responses. A parent who is sensitive to the child's distress may take issue with a spouse for being overly harsh or demanding toward the
child or for not providing accommodation when the child requests it. Conversely,
a parent who is frustrated by the child's anxiety and impaired functioning and sees
the accommodation as maintaining the problem or as manipulation on the part of
the child may upbraid the other parent for giving in to the child, succumbing to

unreasonable demands, or allowing the child to shirk responsibilities. A later chapter provides some useful tools for addressing intraparental conflict surrounding a child's anxiety, but reducing the accommodation, and even merely having an agreed upon plan of action, can begin to defuse a volatile relationship.

Reducing accommodation can also allow for improved functioning in other areas, as resources are reallocated away from the accommodation toward other goals and objectives. Time that is freed up can be diverted to other things such as a sibling's needs, parent together time, or even simply rest, all of which may have been relegated to a back burner as the need to accommodate commanded the parents' time and energy.

Positive Impact on Siblings

Family accommodation impacts siblings as well as parents, and reducing the accommodation can have direct and indirect benefits for the anxious child's siblings. When the sibling has been participating in the accommodation, the reduction in parental accommodation will often be accompanied by reduction in their accommodation as well. The siblings observe the parents accommodating less, and the anxious child coping with the change, and can feel more emboldened to also decline accommodation. Parents may need to actively guide siblings to reduce their own accommodation or at least to make clear to them that they are not expected or obligated to accommodate. Reducing the sibling's accommodation or giving them permission to do so not only frees up time and energy for them but can also reduce the simmering anger that siblings often feel toward an anxious brother or sister for the impact the anxiety problem is having on their lives. Parents who are accommodating less may also be able to devote more attention to siblings who may have felt neglected or shunted aside by the intense focus on the anxious sibling. In some cases, the anxious child has been forcefully imposing accommodation on siblings, through verbal or physical aggression. Parents who act to protect the victim of the aggression, rather than expecting them to accept it or acquiesce to it, can have a positive impact on the sibling, while also conveying an important message to the anxious child about boundaries of permissible behavior even when coping with anxiety.

Improved Parent–Child Relationship

The relationship between parents and their anxious child can suffer under the strain of excessive accommodation. Parents may feel compelled to provide the accommodation, while also feeling frustrated or aggrieved by the demands placed on them. The child may feel guilty about causing the parents distress and react to the feeling with additional problematic behaviors, or by clinging to parents, or asking them repeatedly to confirm their love, all of which place additional strain on the parent–child relationship. When a child uses force or aggression to induce parents to accommodate the unhealthy coercion exacts an extra toll from the parent–child relationship, beyond the need for the accommodation itself. Furthermore, a child who is able to forcefully impose accommodation on parents may begin to use similar methods to achieve other desired goals. It is not uncommon for a child who has compelled parents to accommodate through use of force to attempt to also impose other demands that do not stem directly from the anxiety disorder. In some cases, these additional attempts at coercion reflect the child's need to reaffirm their ability to control parental behavior, because any sign of "mutiny" may also be taken as signal that the prospect of ongoing accommodation is in jeopardy. In other cases, the additional coercive behaviors merely reflect the child learning, and utilizing, an effective tool for achieving things that they want. Either way, a therapist who is able to help parents effectively reduce accommodation and restore healthier parent–child dynamics will be improving the overall parent–child relationship, beyond the reduction in child anxiety. Parents who have successfully reduced accommodation through therapeutic intervention report lower parenting stress and more satisfaction with their relationship with the child.

Increase Child Motivation for Treatment

As discussed earlier, high levels of family accommodation can lead to lower motivation for treatment on the part of the child. While the accommodation is present the child is continually faced with a choice between relying on accommodation to avoid facing their anxiety, or learning to cope more independently with the help of a therapist. Reducing the accommodation means that the child is faced with a new set of choices. Continuing to avoid facing the anxiety is no longer an easy alternative. Now the child must choose between learning to cope with the help of a therapist or facing the anxiety on their own. In this new situation, the child's motivation to get help from a therapist is often significantly increased.

Dealing With Accommodation in Child Anxiety Treatment

5

Assessing Family Accommodation

Evaluating childhood anxiety disorders should always include assessment of family accommodation. This chapter provides guidelines and tools for the initial assessment of accommodation. The following chapter will then detail methods of comprehensively mapping accommodation in treatment and for continually monitoring accommodation throughout the therapeutic process.

INTERVIEWS

Listening for Accommodation

Clinical interviewing can be used to gauge the degree and types of accommodations being provided in cases of childhood anxiety disorders. An astute clinician will begin "listening for accommodation" before any direct queries about accommodation have even been posed. From the first "Tell me why you're here" or "Describe your child's problems," the clinical ear is attuned to descriptions that will usually convey not only the child's individual symptoms, but also the impact those symptoms have on other family members.

> THERAPIST: *Tell me about Jim. What are some of the great things about him, and what are your concerns that bring you in to see me?*
>
> LECK: *Jim's a great kid. He's sensitive, kind, funny. Ever since he was a baby he was always making people laugh. When his sister was dating her boyfriend (now, husband), he was still a little boy. Her boyfriend would come to the house with her and go to his room to play with him. He would say, "Make your faces," and Jim would pull lots of funny faces and make him laugh. That's who he is. Now he's 12, and we worry that that spark, that humor that always filled him and the house, is gone. He's been dealing with anxiety for at least two years. At first, when he started asking about death and dying, we thought it was just a natural phase, of him growing up and learning about death. We explained it to him as best we could, but he didn't seem satisfied. He kept comping back to the topic and asking about it again and again.*

What happens when we die? Where do we go? Will he die? Will we die? How do we know we won't die today? Time after time we thought we had provided the answers he needed and that now he would stop thinking about it, but the next day, sometimes even the same day, he would be back with more questions. Or the same questions all over again. Both of us were also anxious as kids so we thought we understood what he was going through . . . but this was different. It was like his brain just wouldn't quit, and it felt like the time between these conversations was just getting shorter. When he said he thought about killing himself about a year ago, we couldn't believe it. This kid was consumed by fears about death and now he wants to kill himself?? One night we heard a noise from his room, and we found him sitting on the floor near his bed just trembling. He was sitting there in his underwear and just shaking all over. I can't get the look in his eyes out of my mind—like a scared animal. Since then he's had more episodes like that, but he won't talk about them. This year he got a new worry. He thinks he'll throw up, and he doesn't want to. We only realized what was going on when we noticed he wasn't eating his dinner. At first, we thought it was about losing weight, he's always been a little chubby, and we know he gets teased about it sometimes. But he said no, he's not trying to lose weight. He just doesn't want to eat because he might be sick. I'm not sure what scares him so much about that, but it's only gotten worse. When he wouldn't eat we tried giving him soft foods, things that we told him would not make him be sick. It didn't make much sense, but it seemed to help. But he's gotten totally stuck. He'll only eat food that we prepare. Nothing outside, or even bought. We always make sure there are soft foods at every meal, and before he'll taste anything he'll ask us if it can make him throw up. The school nurse called to ask why he isn't eating lunch. We didn't know how much to tell her, so we just said he has a toothache that we're dealing with. I don't know if she bought that. . . . It was sort of absurd because he hadn't been eating in school for a while. He'll come home hungry and asking to eat, but then when he's about to eat he'll stop, and we can see his brain working. He'll ask whether he'll get sick. Where the food came from? Who made it? And lots of other questions. He's starving, but he'll wait until we've given all the right answers before putting anything in his mouth. We're worried that his growth and physical strength will be affected. He just never seems relaxed anymore. He was the funniest guy in the world, and now he never even smiles. I almost miss the time when he was worried about death because at least he could eat, and we knew he was healthy. We need a lifeline.

Jim is presenting with a lot of anxiety. His mood is clearly impacted, and he may be becoming depressed, a common co-morbidity that often follows the onset of anxiety. His eating is disrupted as well, and his parents are obviously very concerned for him. A clinician hearing about Jim's symptoms may start to formulate hypotheses about the most relevant diagnoses, such as generalized anxiety disorder or emetophobia (specific phobia of vomiting). And after further assessment, a treatment plan could be shaped, including cognitive-behavioral therapy for Jim's anxiety and possible depression.

But in hearing about Jim's problems, the therapist should also be noting the various forms of family accommodation that Leck is describing:

- *"Time after time we thought we had provided the answers he needed and that now he would stop thinking about it, but the next day, sometimes even the same day, he would be back with more questions."*
- *"He'll only eat food that we prepare. Nothing outside, or even bought."*
- *"We always make sure there are soft foods at every meal."*
- *"Before he'll taste anything, he'll ask us if it can make him throw up."*
- *"He'll wait until we've given all the right answers before putting anything in his mouth."*

Even without being asked any direct questions explicitly probing accommodation, Leck is providing very important information about a critical aspect of Jim's anxiety problem. Jim's parents have responded to his anxiety as most parents would, providing reassurance when he was worried and making changes they realized were necessary to allow him to eat. In doing so, they have become accustomed to both active participation in Jim's symptom-driven behaviors (when answering his questions about death or about food), and to making major modifications to the family's routines and schedules (when resorting to only eat at home or to prepare all their food rather than buy it).

A therapist who misses these clues or chooses to focus on Jim's symptoms as individual "Jim-only" behaviors and ignores the ways in which his parents are accommodating is overlooking an aspect of the presenting complaint that is just as important as the symptoms themselves. As therapists become more attuned to listening for and hearing about accommodation, it becomes increasingly easy to formulate a more complete picture of Jim's anxiety disorder. And the importance of factoring family accommodation into a comprehensive treatment plan becomes progressively more evident.

Asking about Accommodation

A comprehensive clinical interview should also include more direct assessment of family accommodation. Most parents will not be familiar with the term *family accommodation* prior to treatment. While it may be useful to introduce this term early on and begin the process of psychoeducation regarding the role of family accommodation in childhood anxiety disorders, it is not imperative that parents learn or use this terminology to assess for family accommodation. Instead, the therapist can begin by formulating questions with colloquial words to investigate the impact the anxiety has had on family life. Box 5.1 provides a list of sample questions.

Box 5.1

ASKING PARENTS ABOUT THEIR RESPONSES TO THEIR CHILD'S
ANXIETY SYMPTOMS

- *So tell me about how Jim's anxiety has affected each of you.*
- *What do you do when you see that Jim is feeling anxious or upset?*
- *Does it ever feel like Jim's anxiety causes you to do things differently than before?*
- *What are some of the things you've tried to help Jim overcome his anxiety? Have they worked, even for a while?*
- *How much of your time is taken over by needing to help Jim cope with his problems?*
- *Has your personal space been affected by Jim's problems? Do you ever feel like you have less privacy? Or less space to yourself?*
- *Are there things Jim needs you to do for him, because of the way he feels?*
- *Tell me some of the things you would do differently if Jim was feeling better.*
- *Is it harder for you to get work done?*
- *Do you make special plans because you know Jim is so anxious?*
- *How much time do you think you spend on helping Jim to feel better?*
- *Do you shop differently because of Jim's anxiety? Is there anything special that you buy for him?*
- *Have you ever felt like Jim's anxiety is contagious? Like it makes you anxious as well?*
- *Have any of your friends commented on Jim's anxiety? What have they noticed?*
- *Have you had to cancel plans you made?*
- *What does it feel like for you when Jim is upset or scared?*
- *Do you ever get annoyed with Jim's problems? What do you do then? How does that make you feel?*
- *Have you ever tried to prevent Jim from "giving into" to his fears? How did you do that? What happened when you tried?*
- *Has anyone else tried to talk to Jim about these problems? What did they say? How did he respond?*
- *Are there things you do differently with Jim, compared to his brothers or sisters?*

The examples provided here are just some of the ways a therapist can introduce the topic of family accommodation. By asking open-ended questions, parents may be prompted to share important information that would not be accessible otherwise. It is important to maintain an open, empathic, and nonjudgmental attitude throughout this process. Parents who feel judged, criticized, or blamed may be less likely to speak candidly. Many parents approach the evaluation with the fear that they will be blamed for their child's problems. It is no secret that the field of mental health has a rich history of parent-blaming and parent-shaming. Mothers in particular have been frequently accused of causing their children's emotional disabilities due to ignorant or even malignant behaviors. Even without these misguided and empirically gratuitous theories, parents often believe they contribute to their child's struggles and, consequently, blame themselves (or each other). Often, parents respond to inquiries about their own behaviors with confessions of guilt: "I know we've made lots of mistakes"; "I'm sure I've only made things worse"; or even "This is my fault, I should have known better." These sentiments, rather than motivating a parent to modify their behavior, will often engender discouragement and despair, especially when reinforced by an insensitive therapist.

A neutral attitude, expressed by a therapist who wishes to understand a child's problem rather than to assign blame for the problem, is more productive. When parents feel guilty for having provided family accommodation, it may be useful to share two simple and reassuring facts consistently supported by empirical data: **Virtually all parents accommodate anxious children, and, in general, parents who accommodate often are the same parents who show wonderful and desirable qualities in their parenting behavior**. Caring, sensitive, and enthusiastic parents who take an interest in their child, praise them for doing well, and wish to support them when they are struggling tend to provide a lot of accommodation. A therapist could say with a smile:

- *You're guilty of accommodation? You mean when your child was suffering you wanted to help her? How awful . . .*
- *Parents always accommodate children who are anxious. It's what we're programmed to do!*
- *Frankly, I'd be concerned about a parent who had a child as anxious as yours, and it hadn't impacted them at all.*
- *Don't worry, I probably would've done the same thing.*

Parents may be correct in that assuming their behavior has contributed to growing anxiety in their child, but this outcome does not nullify the endeavors they have made. It would be pointless and cruel to turn all of a parent's efforts to help a child into mere mistakes or to label the sacrifices they have made as futile.

- *You've made tremendous sacrifices on behalf of your child. I admire that.*
- *I don't think any parent could have done more. We'll try to harness all that energy with productive tools.*
- *You did the best you could with what you knew at the time. Nobody could ask for more than that.*
- *These things haven't helped, so we'll try some new ones. But I respect what you've been trying to do.*
- *Your child is fortunate to have parents who love him/her as much as you do and are willing to work so hard for him/her. I think that's going to be really important in overcoming this problem.*

Asking about Accommodation "Hot Spots"

Family accommodation can occur at any time or place, but certain points in the day tend to be particularly susceptible to accommodation. Mealtimes, bedtime, transitions, separations, showers, and homework are all fertile ground for family accommodation. The therapist can follow up with more general questions by asking specifically about these "hot spots" for family accommodation. Open-ended questions, such as those previously described in (Box 5.1), are useful in eliciting the accommodations that are most typical of the parent. But oftentimes additional probing will help them recall other accommodations that were not foremost in their minds on the day of the evaluation. There may also be behaviors that the parent does not recognize as accommodation. This can occur when the parent does not connect the behavior to the child's anxiety and instead sees it as the result of some other problem or as a characteristic of the particular child. Parents can also become so accustomed to accommodating that they forget what behavior is atypical or how they would behave differently if the child was less anxious. Accommodations can become so ingrained in the family culture that it simply becomes "how we do things." Asking for further descriptions of these accommodation "hot spots" can often help to reveal such unrecognized accommodations.

Ask for Details

When parents do describe an accommodating behavior, the therapist should aim to have as complete a description of the accommodation as possible. Understanding the interaction between parent and child and the details of parent accommodating behavior will help inform treatment planning and prevent mistakes down the road. For example, if parents say they answer "many" phone calls a day, the therapist can inquire clarification of the word *many*. In asking this, the therapist should avoid framing questions in a way that may lead to biased answers or feelings of embarrassment from the parent regarding the extent of accommodation. Rather than asking "Is it more than 10 calls?" the therapist could ask, "About how many calls do you think you get a day from the child?" or "Is it closer to 10? Twenty? A hundred?" and then continue the investigation by asking about the content of the calls, the duration of calls, and so forth.

- *If we had a video of your child's bedtime, what would it look like?*
- *Try to give me the play by play. It will help me to understand what your child is experiencing, and what you're facing.*
- *Could you take some notes next time it happens and bring them back so we can go over them together?*
- *Could you keep a log of these events, so we have good data to work with?*

Ask about Each Parent Separately

Children behave differently with different parents, and parents respond differently as well. It is useful to ask about each parent's accommodation separately to avoid argument and prevent parents from blaming each other.

Ask about Sibling Accommodation

Earlier chapters emphasized the role of siblings, as well as parents, in family accommodation of anxious children. The therapist can ask the parents how they think their child's anxiety is impacting their other children. More specific questions about accommodation by siblings can follow. If parents do describe sibling accommodation, it is useful to understand what motivates the sibling to accommodate. Are they accommodating willingly? Or are they doing so under duress? And if siblings are accommodating unwillingly, who is exerting the pressure on them to accommodate? Is it the anxious child or the parents demanding that the sibling accommodate? Even when not directly accommodating, siblings' lives may be impacted by their brother's or sister's anxiety, and it is helpful to ask parents whether they believe this is the case and, if so, how.

Ask the Child as Well as the Parents

Therapists and researchers tend to focus almost exclusively on parental report of family accommodation. However, studies that examine children's perceptions of family accommodation indicate that anxious children are usually aware of their parents' accommodation and can provide useful information beyond what parents report. Parents' understanding of their own accommodating behavior is inherently subjective and can be inaccurate due to bias or misunderstanding. For example, a parent may believe that a certain behavior is an accommodation of their child's anxiety, but the child may feel the parent is accommodating excessively. This happens frequently when a child, whose anxiety causes parents to take up an accommodation, outgrows the fear or overcomes it. Without parents realizing it, that accommodation no longer becomes necessary. Parents can also be unaware that a certain request or demand from their child is driven by anxiety, thus failing to report that behavior as an accommodation. Discussing accommodation with the child also helps to set the stage for later work in reducing accommodation, as the child becomes more aware of it in their anxiety disorder.

RATING SCALES

A number of rating scales have been developed for assessing things like family accommodation, levels of parental interference, and the consequences of unaccommodated children. These rating scales are not a substitute for more in-depth clinical inquiry; the data they provide are limited by necessity. However, they are useful indicators of the degree of family accommodation, offer a comparison across families and time points, and provide parents with evidence-based feedback.

Whenever possible, it is preferable to employ a multi-informant assessment strategy, administering the accommodation scale to both parents and the child. Comparisons of child and parent ratings of family accommodation have revealed significant concordance as well as differences between raters. Likewise, research indicates that parents and children provide significantly different ratings regarding the severity of the child's anxiety symptoms. The previously described biases and misperceptions in the context of clinical interviewing with parents and children equally apply to systematic ratings. Divergent ratings provided by different informants can pose a challenge to the clinician, who will need to integrate the contradicting information to form an accurate clinical picture. At the same time, however, these ratings provide useful and rich information that can ultimately enhance that picture.

The first and most widely used measure of accommodation in childhood anxiety disorders is the **Family Accommodation Scale–Anxiety** (FASA; Lebowitz et al., 2013, 2015). FASA has been used in numerous studies and has proven to have excellent psychometric properties including internal consistency, test–retest reliability, and convergent and divergent validity. There are both parent- and child-rated versions of FASA (Appendixes A and B, respectively), and research indicates moderate agreement between parents and children in accommodation ratings. FASA includes nine items that query different kinds of accommodations and are rated for the frequency with which they occur; for example, "How often did you reassure your child?" (parent version) or "How often did your parent reassure you (like tell you that you don't need to worry, tell you something is OK)?" (child version). The scores for each of the nine accommodation items are summed to achieve an overall measure of family accommodation. Two subscale scores can also be calculated, for participation and modification (described in Chapter 1 of this volume). Factor analyses and confirmatory factor analysis have supported this two-factor structure of participation and modification.

In addition to the nine accommodation items, FASA also includes one question that queries the degree to which providing accommodation causes the parents distress and three items that probe short-term negative child consequences of not accommodating, including the child becoming distressed, more anxious, or angry/abusive.

Finally, the child version of FASA includes three additional items not included in the parent version. These items ask the child to rate the degree to which they believe that the parents' accommodation helps them to feel less anxious in the short-term, the degree to which they believe that continued accommodation will make them less anxious in the future, and the degree to which they believe that parents ought to accommodate less. Analysis of these items in a sample of anxious children indicated that children acknowledge that accommodation is only helpful in the short-term and will not lead to less anxiety in the future. On the other hand, they do not agree that their parents ought to accommodate less.

Because FASA takes very little time to complete and is sensitive to changes in accommodation that occur over the course of therapy, it provides a useful tool for tracking accommodation over time and for evaluating treatment-related changes.

The **Family Accommodation Checklist and Interference Scale** (FACLIS; Thompson-Hollands et al., 2014) was designed to identify the forms of accommodation provided to an anxious child and to gauge the degree of interference caused by the family accommodation. FACLIS includes a list of 20 specific forms of accommodation, and parents are asked to rate the degree of personal and family interference caused by those provided. The number of accommodations that parents agree they provide is taken as a measure of overall accommodation, and the interference ratings provide indications of the associated burden on parents and family.

The **Pediatric Accommodation Scale** (PAS; Benito et al., 2015) is a semistructured interview that requires a trained clinician to administer. The interviewer presents 14 questions about various kinds of accommodation, with questions being further elaborated on through a series of examples that can be tailored to the specific family being assessed. Accommodations are rated for the frequency with which they occur and for the severity of interference they cause. A parent-rated version of PAS is also available and includes five items, each followed by illustrative examples, and rated for frequency and interference.

Instruments specific to obsessive-compulsive disorder (OCD) have also been developed including the Family Accommodation Scale (Pinto, Van Noppen, & Calvocoressi, 2013), the OCD Family Functioning Scale (Stewart et al., 2011), and the Coercive-Disruptive Behavior Scale for Pediatric OCD (Lebowitz, Omer, & Leckman, 2011). This last instrument is unique in its focus on the forceful and coercive imposition of accommodation on parents and family members that is typical of some children with OCD.

The interview techniques and rating scales described here can provide an initial assessment of the degree of accommodations being provided and the degree of impairment they engender. The next chapter includes a method for creating a comprehensive "accommodation map" to more thoroughly identify the various accommodations and to facilitate crafting a treatment plan focused on one or more of the accommodations.

6

Addressing Accommodation

The current chapter begins the "deep dive" into the work of addressing and reducing accommodation in cases of childhood anxiety disorders. This chapter includes suggestions for explaining to parents and children the rationale behind targeting family accommodation, creating an accommodation map that describes the accommodations currently being provided, and selecting an area of focus or specific accommodation to reduce. The next two chapters will discuss how to increase parental supportive responses to child anxiety and how to craft effective plans for actually reducing accommodation. The two following two example cases illustrate the implementation of these processes.

EXPLAINING THE RATIONALE FOR TARGETING FAMILY ACCOMMODATION

While some parents may welcome parent work, others may wonder why a child psychologist is trying to work with them rather than, or in addition to, their child. Parents open to meeting with their child's therapist may still be taken aback by the focus on their own behaviors and expect that the therapist wishes to keep them up-to-date regarding their child's therapy or to offer emotional support. Orienting parents to the importance of addressing family accommodation and to the goal of modifying their own behaviors can play a key role in successful intervention around family accommodation.

As discussed in an earlier chapter, parents may also feel apprehensive about being criticized by the therapist and wary of being "weighed, measured, and found wanting." These sentiments also need to be dealt with, and hopefully eliminated, for a productive therapeutic alliance to ensue. The following discussion offers some suggestions for introducing the topic of family accommodation, making use of metaphors that can be easily understood by parents. Metaphors can be powerful tools in therapy and are often used in the treatment of anxiety. Therapists treating anxiety often use metaphors to externalize the anxiety and help a patient to see their anxiety symptoms as an "external force" to be resisted and challenged. In dealing with accommodation metaphors that help parents and children to see the accommodation as a natural and healthy response, but one that ultimately limits the child's ability to cope independently, can likewise be highly useful. These suggestions are neither exhaustive nor exclusive but can be helpful to a therapist seeking to establish a fruitful partnership with parents who feel energized rather than defensive.

TALKING WITH PARENTS

The Hijacking Metaphor

Anxiety disorders are the great hijacker. An anxiety disorder takes healthy, necessary systems and makes them run wild. Each of your child's anxiety symptoms is a great example of this. His body does exactly what it's supposed to when he's anxious—rev up! This is a healthy defense mechanism designed to help him stay safe by giving him the power for fight or flight. But his anxiety disorder has hijacked this system and makes it "turn on" at the wrong moments and much too frequently. Their worried thoughts are exactly the same. Humans have the capacity to worry because it's a great thing to have! Imagine if we needed to wait until a danger was right there happening in front of us to take protective measures to prevent it. That would be terrible, right?—for example, if your kid had to literally see the truck bearing down on him to take precautionary steps when crossing a street or if your house had to be on fire for you to think it might be unwise to play with matches. Terrible! But his anxiety disorder makes him feel like there's always a truck right there. Or like the house is always just about to catch on fire. It's a healthy and literally critical anxiety system, being hijacked by the anxiety disorder. He can't sleep when he's anxious? Of course, he can't! What would be the point of an anxiety system that made us feel all nice and comfy so we cheerfully drifted off to sleep, while catastrophe was striking around us. No, his anxiety is supposed to keep him up, alert and ready for action! But once again the anxiety disorder, that great hijacker, is taking a useful and healthy system and turning it into a problem by making him feel that the catastrophe is always happening. So, he never gets a good night's sleep.

There's another aspect to kids' anxiety response that's just as healthy and beneficial as their body revving up or their thoughts being worried. And anxiety disorders hijack that system as well. When kids are anxious they look for their parents. And they should! Imagine if a three-year-old who was being attacked by a dog thought "I'd better fight this dog off all by myself. Of course, I could cry and let my parents know that I'm in danger, but nah, I'll just deal with it" Good plan? Terrible plan! Kids are supposed to look for their parents— to call them and get their attention when they feel threatened. It's what keeps us alive until we're old enough to actually protect ourselves. A baby who tried to "go it alone" wouldn't get very far, would they? But here comes the anxiety disorder that hijacks this great system, too. So what's a kid who feels threatened or scared all the time going to do? They're going to look for their parents all the time. They'll call them, cling to them, yell for them, pester them. Because they've decided they want to be annoying kids who drive people crazy? No, because they're doing exactly what they're programmed to do, what they're supposed to do—which is whatever it takes to trigger the other part of this great system. Because we, parents, are programmed too. We're programmed to notice when our kids are in danger or upset and to help them get safe and feel better. Imagine if the mom of that toddler being attacked by a dog heard her crying out and thought, "Ah, she'll be fine. I could go check on her because she's screaming bloody murder but I think I'll take a nap instead." Not exactly mom of the year, right? We are the opposite way. Some parents feel like a little part of them hasn't relaxed since their first child was born. Because there's always that preparedness, that sensitivity to notice if our kid needs us. We're supposed to step in when they feel scared. So we do it. But we're just as hijacked as the kid. A child's anxiety disorder takes over this beautiful system of child signaling and parent responding and makes it run wild. Just like the racing heart and thoughts.

And because we're being hijacked, we have to get suspicious. We need to suspect that when these systems are being triggered, it may not be because they're actually needed but because they've been hijacked. We want your child to notice his heart racing and think "I know why this is happening. It's because of my anxiety disorder. I'm not in danger. And I don't need to do anything to stay safe. I just need to wait a bit and I'll calm down." When he starts thinking like that he's half way to being done with the anxiety disorder. And we need you to be suspicious as well. We need you to suspect that when your child is pushing your sensitive-parent role button it's not because they actually need you to step in and help. It's because the great hijacker is back. In fact, if you do step in, your child is not going to think, "I just need to wait and I'll be calm" or "I wasn't really in any danger to begin with." They're going to think, "Thanks, Mom, you really saved me there! I hope I can rely on you to do it again next time."

Independent Coping

Children are lucky because they have two systems for coping with anxiety. They have an independent system, where they learn to regulate their emotions and "get back to calm." And they have an attachment system where they can use a parent to "get back to calm." This is great because it means they don't always have to calm themselves. And, at first, children rely pretty heavily on the attachment system. It's really powerful. Just being near a parent, or seeing them, even just hearing their voice can bring a child back to calm. It's like when a small child falls and parents give them a kiss to make them feel better. If someone was studying human behavior scientifically, they might conclude that parents' lips secrete painkillers. What's really happening, of course, is that a tender kiss from a parent is an attachment signal. It helps to calm us down and can make us feel better. Over time, kids usually start to make more use of their independent systems. Teenagers don't usually want a kiss when they fall. They do other things. Like rubbing where it hurts, distracting themselves, hopping about, or just waiting for it to pass. It's the same with fear. Over time, kids start to make more use of their independent ability to calm down. They may not hop about as with a stubbed toe, but they find other ways to distract themselves, or they talk themselves down, or they take some deep breaths, or sometimes they just wait for it to pass.

For some kids, this shift is really hard and they need help. They're anxious so much of the time, and their independent coping systems may not work quite as well. And so they continue to rely on the attachment system by being near parents, listening to their voices, and relying on them to make things better. It's not that these kids don't have an independent coping system; it just needs some practice. It's like someone who is born with a weakness in their legs and falls a lot and so prefers not to walk around too much. What they really need is the opposite. It's not that they don't have legs. Or even that their legs can't get stronger. It's just harder for them and comes less naturally. We want to encourage someone like that to walk every day! By not walking, their legs will just get weaker and weaker. But if they start practicing, they can catch up. They may never run a marathon, but they can be just as capable as everyone else. And who knows, with enough practice, maybe they will run that marathon. We don't want to carry them around or push them in a wheelchair. That doesn't help; it keeps them weak. We want to encourage them to walk, and when they ask for that wheelchair, we want to stay firm and say, "No way!" When they think they can't do it, we want to encourage them, show them we believe in them, and, above all, keep them walking. Even if they think we're being mean, we know we're doing the right thing. An anxious child has an independent coping system just like all the other kids. It's just a little weaker and needs extra practice. So when we accommodate, it's a little bit like giving them that wheelchair. It helps them to feel good but keeps them weak. I want to help you do the opposite. Show them that you believe in them. Let them know that you care and that you know how hard it is. Encourage them to find that strength that's in there, and soon they'll be getting back to calm all on their own.

The Avoidance Trap

Everybody wants to avoid the things that make them anxious. Well, sometimes we enjoy things that make us anxious like scary rides and horror movies. But we only enjoy them when we know we're actually safe. When we're sure things are OK it can be fun to be a little scared. But if a roller coaster breaks down, nobody's having fun anymore. Everyone wants off. Because real anxiety, actually feeing unsafe and not knowing if things will turn out OK, is not fun, and we want to avoid it. Whether it's situations that scare us or just feelings of threat and insecurity, being anxious will make us want to avoid and feel safe again. But avoidance is also a trap. If we avoid things, we stay scared of them. We don't get used to them or realize they're actually safe. In fact, we become even more scared every time we avoid them. It's like we're telling ourselves: "See I avoided that, it must really be dangerous just like I thought. And I'm only safe now because I avoided it, otherwise it would have been a disaster." It's easy to keep believing that when we continue to avoid. As we avoid, we get more anxious, and as we get more anxious, we avoid more and more. We learn to take extra-special steps to make sure we don't even come near the thing we're avoiding. We become super avoiders. And, of course, we pay a steep price in all the things we can't do. But it feels like it's worth it to be safe! We also start relying on our parents for help in avoiding. All those little and big ways that parents can help a child avoid the things that make them anxious: doing things for them, checking to eliminate doubt, reassuring them, clearing a path like a minesweeper removing anxiety mines so that nothing sets them off. Those can all feel like help, but they're keeping that avoidance trap going. When our parents are our minesweepers, we don't really get a chance to discover that those weren't really mines at all—that we wouldn't have exploded, we would have just been uncomfortable for a while. We don't get used to all those things our parents are helping us not do. In fact, with help from family we can really be amazing avoiders, but we're not getting any less anxious because we're stuck in the avoidance trap.

Actions Speak Louder Than Words

The therapist can introduce this concept by posing the question: What would you want most for your Clara to know? This kid, who is so scared of embarrassing herself and of what others will think about her. If you could tell her one thing, and she would really accept it, just know deep down that it's definitely true, what would you tell her? That she's great just as she is? That it doesn't matter what other people think? That she's not going to humiliate herself in front of everyone? Maybe that people aren't quite as obsessed with thinking about her and judging her as she thinks? Wouldn't it be great if you could get her to realize even one of those things? If you had the power to do that? Sounds amazing! Certainly, you wouldn't want to tell her the opposite. That's obvious. I'm sure you don't say to her, "Listen Clara, before you go into class you ought to know there's a good chance you're going to really mess up, and I bet everyone will laugh at you and talk about it for ages." Who would say that? Or "Hey, Clara, you know that school trip you've been worrying about? Well, it turns out you were right. All the other kids are just waiting to pounce on you because you speak too fast. Or too slow. Or tell stupid jokes. Basically, nobody really likes you anymore." Or even "Oh, Clara? Remember how you told me you thought you would die if everyone saw you blushing because it's just too humiliating? Well . . . yup. You might not actually die, but you'll never be the same again. You'll just feel worse and worse and that terrible awful feeling will never go away." Of course, you'd never say any of those horrible things! I know you wish you could show her the opposite. That her thoughts are irrational, and exaggerated, and absurd. But Clara is not just listening to your words. In fact, your words don't actually make that big of a difference. If they did, well, you'd already have told her how to feel and things would be fine. Clara is listening to what you do. When your words say, "The trip will be fine," but your actions say, "I'm not sure you can do this," she only hears the uncertainty and doubt. And when your words say, "Nobody will laugh at you," but you plead with her teacher never to call on her, your actions are saying, "You can't handle this." When you leave places early because she's getting uncomfortable you can tell her the whole ride home that she could have stayed, but she's already listened to your action saying, "I know you actually couldn't."

Each of these examples illustrates a different approach to the topic of family accommodation, and many therapists have their own variations or preferred way of introducing the topic with parents. What all good approaches will share is an empathy for the parents' dilemma, a lack of judgement for accommodations that have been provided in the past, and a relatable rationale for reducing accommodation as a means of helping their anxious child.

TALKING WITH CHILDREN

Work with parents can be done independently of child therapy or alongside and coordinated with child therapy. Some therapists prefer not to work with the child and parents at the same time, while others feel that working with both allows for synergy and integration. When there is opportunity to do so, it can be useful to explain to children the rationale for focusing on the family accommodation. The topic can be broached either in a joint session with the child and parents present or, in cases where clinical judgement suggests it would be preferable, in sessions with the child alone. The goal here is not necessarily to convince the child that they will be better off if the accommodation is reduced. This would be a good outcome, and, in fact, many children already know or sense this, but it is not critical that they be persuaded or that they acknowledge it if they are convinced. Rather, the goals are to create a framework within which the child can understand the actions the parents will take; to provide support for the parents by demonstrating that they will be acting on expert advice (and sometimes to allow the child to direct anger or blame toward the therapist rather than the parents); to open up communication and discussion in the family of a topic that may have been avoided previously; to clarify that the changes are being made with the child's well-being in mind and not only for parents' sake; to acknowledge that the process can be difficult for the child and that this is not taken lightly; to invite feedback from the child that can help to shape treatment plans; and to express confidence that the child is able to cope and will ultimately get better as a result of the parent' actions.

> It sounds like your anxiety has been really bad recently, and you've been really brave coping with it all this time. I'm glad you're here now so we can help. We've been talking about some of the things we can do together to help you get better, and I think you're going to do great! I'm also going to be talking to your mom and dad about some ways that they can help you as well. They love you a lot and really want to do everything they can. I'm going to think with them about

which things they're doing right and which things they should probably be doing differently. That's always how it works: Kids come here to learn, and parents come here to learn as well. For example, we talked about how because television characters make you really uncomfortable, your parents have stopped letting your sister watch her shows. That's one we need to think about. Of course, it makes sense that you prefer she not see something that scares you, and your parents want to help you with that. But sometimes the things we do to help actually don't really help. Can you think of something you used to be scared of and now you're not anymore? I bet that's because you kept on doing it, or facing it. What would have happened if your parents had said, "OK, that's over now, no more of that ever again"? I bet you'd still be pretty scared. So, we'll think really hard about this and try to come up with some things that are actually more helpful. I guarantee we won't be trying to surprise you. In fact, let me say that to your parents right here in front of you: No surprises! We're going to let you know the plan every step of the way. I can't promise that you'll like all of my suggestions, but I can promise that they won't hurt you. And if anything that I recommend makes you too uncomfortable or makes you mad at me, you can always tell me that. I won't get mad back! I like it when kids tell me how they really feel, so don't hold back. We may even make some changes based on what you say. Maybe not always, but nobody's perfect, I can make mistakes, and you might have some really good ideas I'll want to use.

MAPPING ACCOMMODATION

Even after good and thorough evaluation, there are likely to be accommodations that have not been discussed. As the therapist comes closer to choosing an accommodation to modify (discussed next), it is better to have more information about the current accommodations. Mapping out the accommodation can take an entire session (or even more) and is followed by parents monitoring their behavior for such accommodations over the course of one week. This time is crucial as it yields valuable information and helps develop better treatment targets.

A straightforward method for mapping accommodation is to review a typical day in the child's and parents' life. Starting as early as the parent wakes up, the therapist can ask the parents to describe in detail what they consider a typical day and to note any changes they have made to their behavior due to their child's anxiety. The review can focus particularly on the accommodation "hot spots" described in Chapter 5, such as mealtime, showers, bedtime, transitions, separations, and homework. The therapist can ask questions when a behavior or pattern described sound as though they may reflect family accommodation. For example:

THERAPIST: *Let's go through what a day looks like for you and Theo. Start from the moment you wake up and try to describe for me how things go throughout the day. I know not every day is the same but think about a typical day, and if there are accommodations you only do on some days, let me know about*

> those as well. I'd like each of you to tell me the things you do, which, of course, are going to be different, as well as the things Theo does.
>
> VIVIENNE: Well, I get up around 5:45 and I get dressed. I'll usually wake Theo around six.
>
> THERAPIST: Is it hard to wake Theo up?
>
> VIVIENNE: Not at all. He's always been a morning person. Sometimes he's already awake when I go in, but usually I just touch his head or call him softly and he'll be up.
>
> THERAPIST: OK, thanks. I envy you! Six is pretty early. Does he need to get up at that time to make the school bus?
>
> ENRIQUE: Not really, he just . . .
>
> VIVIENNE: I was answering him, you know. Anyway, it's true. He doesn't really need to be up at six. But he likes to take his time in the morning. He's very particular about his clothes and his hair.
>
> ENRIQUE: [Mumbles]
>
> VIVIENNE: Enrique, please! He's particular. I used to wake him at 6:30, but he would spend so much time choosing his clothes and asking me if he looked bad that it would make him late. For a while I was picking out his clothes for him, to try to make it easier. And because I have great taste [laughs].
>
> THERAPIST: But now he chooses by himself?
>
> VIVIENNE: Yes, he told me he prefers it that way, but he still asks me many times if he's making a mistake with one piece of clothing or another. He also brushes his teeth for a long time. He says he doesn't want people to think he has bad breath. Who ever heard of a teenage boy who worries so much about his teeth?
>
> THERAPIST: It sounds like that all takes a lot of time. Go on.
>
> VIVIENNE: Yes, so eventually I started waking him up earlier so he has time for all his clothes and his tooth brushing and his questions, and everything.

In this snippet of dialogue between a therapist and two parents, going through the day has immediately yielded valuable information. Vivienne is accommodating her son Theo by waking him at least half an hour early each day because he is anxious about his appearance and his odor. She also answers many questions about his clothing and, in the past, accommodated by selecting the clothing for him.

The conversation is also beginning to hint at some additional information that may require further exploration and attention if the parent work is to be successful. There appears to be some tension between the two parents, due to their differing attitudes about Theo's behavior. Vivienne normalizes the behavior, labeling Theo as "particular," and seems to be downplaying its importance and the extent of accommodation. Enrique, though he does not clearly express his views in this brief interaction, gives the impression that he does not quite see things the same way. Disagreement between parents of anxious children, with regards to the child's symptoms and the parental response, is common and can pose a challenge to effective parent work. Chapter 9 offers suggestions for addressing parental discord and improving collaboration in addressing family accommodation.

In mapping the accommodation, the therapist may wish to ask parents to also describe a weekend day in addition to a school day as these can be very different. Different amounts of time spent together, different activities, and different goals and objectives for the child can all contribute to a very different picture of family accommodation as well.

Finally, the accommodation map should include accommodation by siblings, teachers, or others in the child's circle who may be providing accommodation.

The therapist can give the parents the Accommodation Monitoring Chart and ask them to monitor their behavior over the course of the week, noticing and noting down when they are providing accommodation. Parents can note the frequency and circumstances of the accommodations identified in the mapping out process and can also make note of other accommodations that are either new or were not identified previously.

CHOOSING WHERE TO FOCUS

Most family's accommodation map will include several, and often many, different accommodations. It won't be possible for parents to change their behavior in all these domains at once, nor is it likely to be beneficial to the child for the parents to completely modify their behavior in all areas all at once. The therapist and the parent will therefore have to choose where to focus their efforts, which is not a trivial choice.

One important consideration is the parents' preference and motivation. Parents are more likely to persist with a target that they identified as important—both because they clearly think this is a valuable and important target and because they can feel more ownership and agency around a plan that is based on their preference. Of course, parents may not agree with each other and can have different preferences. Vivienne, for example, may not feel that waking Theo up early is an important accommodation, while Enrique may believe that it is. The therapist can take both perspectives into account and, even while steering toward one or the other's suggestion, can acknowledge the validity of the different thoughts. Having both parents on board will make each of them more likely to persist.

Additional considerations include the frequency of the accommodation, the extent and severity of interference yielded, the child's attitudes and responses when not accommodated, and the potential for deterioration in the child or family functioning upon encountering difficulties with the plan.

Frequent accommodations that occur multiple times per week or per day are preferable because they afford many opportunities for the parents to practice and for the child to become accustomed to the new parental behavior. An accommodation that happens only rarely, even when important in the eyes of the parents, may not occur at all between sessions, making it more difficult to implement a practical plan. A rare accommodation could be selected as an additional target alongside a more frequent one (see Box 6.1).

Box 6.1

SELECTING A TARGET ACCOMMODATION—POINTS TO CONSIDER

- Does this accommodation happen frequently?
- Are parents motivated to reduce this accommodation?
- Does this accommodation interfere with family functioning?
- What do parents think will happen if they reduce this accommodation?
- How does the child feel about reducing this accommodation?

Accommodations that cause significant interference for the parents or other family members are generally preferable for two reasons. First, parents are likely to be motivated to accomplish meaningful change and thus may adhere more resolutely and consistently to the treatment plan. Second, improvement in these accommodations will likely reflect meaningful improvement in the family life, in line with the interference the accommodation was causing.

The potential for deterioration in the child's functioning, when not accommodated, should also be considered carefully. For example, if Vivienne were to not wake up Theo early, or if she stopped answering repeated questions about his clothes and looks in the morning, it may become more likely that Theo would be late for school. Or that one or both of the parents would be late for work due to having to remain with him until he felt able to leave for school. Reducing accommodations around bedtime carry the potential for disrupted sleep, both for the anxious child and for others in the home. Reducing accommodations around mealtimes can lead temporarily to diminished eating. The implication of these risks is *not* that these targets should not be addressed. Every accommodation probably has some potential to impact the child or family functioning in one way or another. Rather, the implication is that these possibilities should be considered, parents should be prepared for them, and the plan that is devised should include contingencies for how parents will respond in the event that they occur, as discussed in the section on devising accommodation reduction plans.

The child's input can also be taken into account in selecting an area of focus. A child may be less resistant to a plan that has taken their preferences into account. And even when their wishes are not ultimately the deciding factor, listening to their view respectfully, and acknowledging their stake in the matter can facilitate an easier process. It may be preferable to start by targeting an accommodation that the child feels willing to take on, even when other accommodations would usually be the first choice. Additional targets can follow, and beginning the process in a collaborative manner is valuable.

7

Parental Support

An Alternative to Family Accommodation

Anxious children who rely heavily on family accommodation can feel as though accommodation is the only way for them to get through days that are infused with anxiety or to cope with the situations they fear. Parents, too, can come to believe that their child's anxiety disorder presents them with only two options: either to accommodate their child or to remain indifferent to his difficulty and suffering. Faced with this choice, it is not surprising that the vast majority of parents elect to accommodate. The choice is made even more difficult by the various pressures and motivations described in earlier chapters, such as the need to maintain the child's, the household's, and their own functioning; the social discomfort that can come from having a child display anxious behavior in public; or the parental belief that experiencing anxiety can have a damaging impact on their child's physical or psychological health. The ongoing accommodation that results from viewing the parental choice this way and from the added pressures that these additional considerations bring to bear on parents, further solidify the child's belief that no alternative to accommodation exists. For the anxious child, to whom the experience of anxiety feels unbearable and intolerable, it is easy to believe that only parental accommodation can reduce the anxiety. This is similar to the way a phobic child may believe that only escaping fearful situations through acts of avoidance will lower the level of distress that they feel and that their anxiety will increase overwhelmingly if not avoided. A child may similarly believe that only accommodation by parents will reduce or prevent their distress and that in the absence of accommodation, their anxiety will engulf them. In this view of themselves, the child is weak and vulnerable, susceptible to anxiety and helpless against it, with parental accommodation as their only line of defense.

Endorsement of this choice between accommodation or indifference has another lamentable result: the belief that a parent who is not accommodating is acting out of a lack of understanding for the child's predicament, at best, or even out of a lack of caring. Children will often express this view explicitly to their parents, making the choice not to accommodate even harder. This belief that only providing accommodation can convey appreciation and compassion for the child's distress contributes to the intrafamilial strife in families of anxious children. When one parent is more willing to accommodate than the other, a child may interpret their different behavior as expressing different levels of love and feel embittered or resentful toward the parent who accommodates less. It can be painful to hear a child express such views, when, in fact, both parents are acting in accordance with their understanding of the child's needs.

Previous attempts by parents to withdraw accommodation may have served to reinforce these views. In the absence of a systematic and deliberate approach and without the help of intervention by a knowledgeable therapist, parents' earlier attempts at not accommodating will typically have been sporadic and inconsistent. Furthermore, these attempts generally have been driven by momentary frustration with the child or by other demands on the parents' time that are not directly related to the child's anxiety. For example, a parent who has already answered a reassurance-seeking question many times over may reach a breaking point at which they angrily declare that they refuse to answer again. This understandable behavior on the parents' side is easily perceived by the child as a punitive act directed against them. After all, if the parent has already answered many times, they have implicitly conveyed their understanding that the child requires these answers to feel reassured. And the angry tone, which reflects merely their exasperation with what feels like a Sisyphean effort at reducing their child's anxiety, can be construed by the child as tacit affirmation that the parents are angry at them for not feeling better.

When Jenna explained to her father, Ronin, how much she hated taking the school bus in the morning, Ronin agreed to take part in a carpool arranged by some of the other parents. But Ronin soon found that rather than being part of the carpool, he was *the carpool. Jenna was almost as anxious about getting picked up by other parents as she was about taking the bus. And so, Ronin ended up repeatedly filling in for the other parents who were happy to be off the hook. When Ronin had an important early meeting at work, he told Jenna the night before that the next day she would be picked up by her best friend's mom. Jenna was adamant: "I can't go with her! You have to take me!" Ronin asked her to be reasonable. He reminded her that he had been going out of his way to help her and explained that now he needed her to "step up" and to think about someone else for a change. Jenna was insulted that her father was calling her selfish and yelled, "You think I want to feel this way? You don't know what it's like for me. You don't care at all." At this point Ronin felt himself losing control. How could she say that to him after everything he was doing for her? "That's it!" he told her, his voice now also rising. "You're going to go with them tomorrow, and from now on, it's either the car pool or the school bus. No more personal chauffeur. Who do you think you are?" The next day, after a difficult morning getting Jenna out of the house that almost led to Ronin being late to his meeting after all, Ronin thought over what he had said. He felt bad for raising his voice, and he reminded himself that Jenna was right; he really didn't know what it was like for her. He had never felt the way she did, after all. When he came*

*home he apologized for yelling at her, and Jenna said she was sorry as well.
"So you'll drive me again? Please, please, please?" Ronin sighed and started
thinking about how to reschedule the next month's morning meeting.*

Ronin is sensitive to Jenna's anxiety. He accepts that she is truly anxious and wants
to help her. His spontaneous attempt to withdraw an accommodation that had become a standard household practice backfired, making him less likely to try again
in the future. Tackling the accommodation without adequate preparation and a
systematic plan made it less likely to succeed. In fact, even though Jenna actually
did get to school without him on the day in question, the end result was a higher
commitment on his part to accommodate in the future and a stronger belief on
Jenna's side that caring and compassionate behavior on her father's part can only
be expressed through accommodation. The fact that the one time he did not accommodate his behavior was accompanied by anger and accusations of selfish-
ness confirmed Jenna's view that not accommodating is a punitive or disciplinary
action. In this context, introducing a plan to systematically reduce accommodation requires a complete reframe of the role of accommodation and of the views
the parents are expressing toward both the child's anxiety and the child's ability to
cope with it. Rather than conveying annoyance with the child or that something
else is more important, changes in accommodation can be framed as a means of
helping the child and as conveying a belief in the child's ability to cope.

SUPPORT = ACCEPTANCE + CONFIDENCE

The therapist can help parents to achieve this reframe by introducing the concept
of *parental support*. Increasing supportive parental responses, before or alongside
active reduction in accommodation, helps both the parents and the child to cope
with the difficult changes they undertake. Support, in the context of childhood
anxiety symptoms, refers to words or actions that tell the child, "We understand
how you feel," and "We know that you can cope." Expressing both of these views
and integrating them into one supportive message can be difficult and may require practice. The therapist can help by explaining the rationale for support, offering examples of supportive statements and behaviors, role-playing supportive
reactions to difficult situations with the child, and pointing out times when the
parents are not being supportive.

The process of implementation begins with listening to how parents describe
their child and their own parenting behaviors. Parents will often provide the therapist with clues to how challenging it is for them to be supportive and the aspects of
support that are hardest for them. By listening for these clues, taking note of them,
and returning to them at an opportune time when working on increasing support,
the therapist is equipped with valuable information that can be harder to access
through direct inquiry. From the first "Tell me about your child," parents will be
describing not only their child's symptoms, but also their own attitudes about
these symptoms and their beliefs about their child's vulnerability and resilience.

THERAPIST: *So, I understand that Luca was diagnosed with generalized anxiety disorder by his pediatrician? Tell me about that.*

MARCO: *Well, Luca's always been very fragile. Even small things can set him off. When he was a toddler, we started to realize he's not like other kids. I would take him to a kind of baby athletics program and would watch all the other kids rushing from one activity to the next, and I'd just feel so jealous of the other parents.*

THERAPIST: *How did Luca behave differently?*

MARCO: *It's like he never wanted to try anything new. If he wasn't sure he could do it perfectly, he would rather not do it at all. He just couldn't handle not being great at something right away. I'd have to push him to try something. I mean, you're a toddler! Who even cares if you can climb up on a pile of mattresses or not, right? I'd be there thinking, you have your whole life to worry about success and failure, do you really need to start now?*

THERAPIST: *And more recently?*

BIANCA: *It's like Marco said, he can't try anything if he's not sure how it will go. And if there's any kind of stress in the environment, he just goes to pieces. Last year there was a boy in his class who had some behavioral issues. The teacher, maybe because she was new, she didn't really know how to handle that other kid and things would get out of hand. Some kids thought it was funny, but Luca . . . it just drove him crazy. If the boy did something wrong and the teacher got angry Luca worried that she would be angry at him next and would be paralyzed with fear that he'll get into trouble. And if the boy got away with things, Luca would drive himself nuts thinking about the injustice of it. He can't cope with knowing that there's any injustice in the world. I think about what will happen when he really learns about the world! It'll crush him.*

MARCO: *He just makes himself sick thinking about things that don't even really affect him at all. The school did a project about poverty and things like that, and Luca just couldn't cope. He would come home crying and he couldn't do anything. He'd want to know exactly why some people are poor and others are not. Or how do we know we won't be poor? He's in sixth grade and he wants to fix the whole world! I've told him a million times, you don't need to think about this stuff. It's not your job. Just go to school, do your project, hang out with friends. Be a kid for god's sake.*

Bianca and Marco are describing some typical behaviors often seen in childhood generalized anxiety disorder. An aversion to novelty, a fear of imperfection and of getting into trouble, a difficulty controlling worrisome thoughts, strong emotional responses to distal events, and a need for reassurance about the future. In listening to the parents speak about Luca, the therapist can also take note of some of the attitudes that may make it harder for them to convey support when confronted with Luca's anxiety. The parents' use of words such as "fragile," "can't cope," "couldn't handle," and "it will crush him" suggest that they will have difficulty expressing confidence in Luca's ability to handle and tolerate anxiety. And note the attitude expressed by Marco, that Luca shouldn't be thinking about the things that worry him and that his worries do not make sense. In early childhood, Marco found it difficult to comprehend that Luca would be apprehensive about his performance, and now that Luca is in the sixth grade, Marco is bewildered by Luca's strong reactions to social injustice or poverty. This pattern suggests that expressing acceptance and validation of Luca's anxiety may come less naturally to Marco.

Marco's and Bianca's reactions to their son's anxiety are not difficult to understand, of course. They are not expressing anything but concern for their child, frustration that he seems to make his own life so much harder than necessary, and a wish that he could feel better and enjoy his childhood more. Marco is confused at Luca's preoccupations, but he does not ridicule or taunt him for them. And when the parents describe Luca as "fragile" or unable to "cope," they are merely describing what they observe. Nevertheless, these terms and beliefs can make supporting Luca more difficult and also influence the way that Luca sees himself. A child who frequently hears himself described as fragile is likely to incorporate this description into his view of himself and come to believe that he cannot, in fact, cope with discomfort. And a child who does feel that their performance matters or is intensely preoccupied with thoughts about something they perceive as being wrong is not able to simply "let it go" because a parent says it is not necessary to think about it.

In some cases, parents may express even less supportive attitudes toward children's emotions. For example, becoming angry at the child for not being "braver" or for being "weak" or even harshly disciplining a child for overly dramatic expressions of fear and distress. In these cases, the work of increasing support takes on an even more vital role and is likely critical to the success of an intervention aimed at reducing family accommodation.

The process of thoroughly mapping the family accommodation, with the therapist asking for detailed descriptions of interactions surrounding each accommodation, serves the additional purpose of providing invaluable information on the parents' response style. Do they convey support for the child? Are they able to explicitly acknowledge that their child is genuinely anxious and to legitimize and validate this emotion? Do they communicate a belief in their child's strength? Do they have such a belief? How similar or different are the two parents' responses? Does one parent convey confidence while the other parent expresses acceptance? Considering these questions can help the therapist to intervene effectively and guide the parents toward more supportive behavior.

We're going to be asking Maleah to handle some difficult things. I am 100% sure that she can do it, and I think you'll see she's a lot stronger than you thought. But if we're going to be asking this of her, we need Maleah to know that she has your support. You're going to show her that by being extra supportive. There's a simple recipe for support. It's an easy recipe to remember because there are just two ingredients. But you can't make support without both ingredients. It's like trying to make mac and cheese but leaving out the macaroni or the cheese. You definitely need both of them! The recipe for support is: "We get that this is hard," and "We know you can handle it." Don't think that Maleah will just know you feel this way. You have to actually tell her. Repeatedly. Maybe you think you've always told her those things. That's great, keep telling her. You can't be too supportive, so don't be afraid to say it again and again.

     Listening to you talk about Maleah before, I noticed you do a lot of ingredient number one. It sounds like you are awesome parents who make sure that Maleah knows you understand what she's going through. For example, you told me that you say things like "It's OK to feel this way" and "It's so hard." And you help her by labeling her emotions when you say things like "Maleah, you're feeling very, very scared right now." That's really great, and I want you to keep on saying those things to her. We're just going to add that second ingredient, so we don't get just mac and mac instead of mac and cheese. So, from now on, how about if every time you say something like "It's so hard," you also add, "You're so strong. I'm sure you can cope," "But we know you'll be OK" or "You can handle it, Maleah, and we're really proud of you." Do you think you can say that to her as well?

When parents struggle to convey empathy for a child's suffering, it may be useful to identify the positive parental motivation that stands in the way of being more supportive. Some parents may be genuinely uncaring, but far more frequently a belief, or attitude, or the parents' own anxiety is impeding the support. For example, if a parent believes that acknowledging their child's anxiety means it is unfair to expect the child to cope, they may be reluctant to express the acknowledgement. Or, a parent may believe that by validating the child's feeling, they are also validating the reality of the child's belief and that if they reject or deny the anxiety, the child will eventually realize there is no need to be afraid. In some cases, what seems like parental reject of what the child is feeling is actually an expression of how the parent wishes the child felt or of how they themselves feel about the worry or concern. For example, when a child says something is frightening, and a parent responds with "No, it's not," they may actually mean "It's not dangerous" rather than "It's not frightening," but from the child's perspective the parent appears to be saying that the child is feeling something silly or that they are not actually feeling scared at all. Frequently, parents simply do not have the words to express support or are not used to speaking to their child in this manner.

The therapist, in identifying the motivation or belief that hinders supportive responses, will find it easier to guide the parent to better express support for their child. Acknowledging the legitimate parental motivation underpinning the behavior, or the positive intentions that drive it, will generally lead to a more productive intervention than responding critically to the lack of current support.

THERAPIST: *Kristen, it sounds like Ian's anxiety is very frustrating to you. I noticed that you've tried many times to tell him things like "It's not so bad"* or "not to make a big deal" out of things. Especially in the morning when it's time to go to school and he gets stomachaches or is feeling nauseous and he wants to stay home from school, it sounds like you try very hard to make him see that school is not a big deal. You told me you've told him a million times that he should just "get it together" or "not carry on about it." But when we were here talking about it without him, you also said you know he really does feel sick and that you've heard him throwing up in the bathroom. I think you're worried that if Ian knows you realize how hard going to school is for him you won't be able to make him go.

KRISTEN: I think if he stays home one day, I'll never get him back to school.

THERAPIST: Right, so you're very careful not to let that happen.

KRISTEN: You think I'm being too hard on him? Should I be letting him stay home once in a while? It would definitely make my mornings easier!

THERAPIST: No, my guess is your instinct is spot on—that staying home will probably just make it harder to go the next day, not easier.

KRISTEN: Exactly, so I need to show him that it's not a big deal. That he's making a mountain out of a mole hill.

THERAPIST: I think we can split those things up. There's the question of how Ian is feeling and then there's the separate question of whether or not he goes to school. We can't make Ian feel like it's easy to go, but we can still make it clear that it's something he has to deal with.

KRISTEN: But won't that make me seem like I don't care about him? If I tell him this is horrible and do it anyway?

THERAPIST: Well, how would you feel if you needed to do something really, really hard—if you had no choice and you had to do it, but you knew it was going to be extremely difficult?

KRISTEN: That's how I feel every morning!

THERAPIST: Exactly! But would it make it easier if I told you it wasn't hard at all. That you're making a mountain out of a mole hill?

KRISTEN: I guess not. I'd think you don't really get it. Do you think that's what I'm doing?

THERAPIST: Not at all! I think it's super hard. And I think you're an amazing mom for keeping him in school every day. That's an impressive accomplishment precisely because it's so hard. And his job is hard too. Telling him it's easy won't make it any easier. You can show him you know it's hard without also letting him stay home. It doesn't mean you're being cruel. It just means you know what he's going through. That way it shows him you are making him go because you believe in him and know it's best for him, not because you think he doesn't have a problem at all. What do you think you could tell him tomorrow morning?

KRISTEN: I guess I could say "Ian, OK, it is a mountain. But you're going to climb that mountain! And you're going to get to the top!"

THERAPIST: I love it! So instead of being a crybaby, now he's a brave mountain climber! That's really good.

SUPPORT IS DIFFERENT FROM ACCOMMODATION

Support differs from accommodation in important ways. The view of the child that is imparted through accommodation and the perspective of the world that is communicated through accommodation differ drastically from those of support. Accommodation can be driven by an acceptance and acknowledgement of the child's distress, but it does not convey to the child that they are able to cope with the anxiety. On the contrary, when parents accommodate their anxious child, they are likely conveying to the child that they believe the opposite, that the child is not able to cope unless accommodated. Parents' actions speak louder than words, and their accommodating behavior is going to overshadow any message of confidence that may verbally accompany the behavior. The message of vulnerability is also likely to be more closely aligned with what the child already believes about themselves, which will further amplify this message through resonance with pre-existing beliefs.

Accommodating behavior also sends the child a very different message about the world or the feared situation than that which is broadcast through supportive parental responses. By providing accommodation, parents are likely to confirm the child's beliefs that the situation they fear is, in fact, dangerous, at least to them if not to everyone. For example, a child who worries about her parents' safety and asks them to avoid rush hour traffic by leaving home or work at special times may take their acquiescence as tacit confirmation that contending with rush hour traffic is, in fact, overly dangerous. In contrast, supportive responses validate that the child is anxious, but do so without also validating that accuracy of the fearful thought. By not allowing the child's anxiety to shape the parental behavior through accommodation, the parents are distinguishing between acknowledging a thought and acknowledging that the thought is correct. Parents may find it difficult at first to make this distinction, between validating a thought and validating the accuracy of the thought. The therapist can help by providing examples of supportive statements and practicing rewording parental statements from protective ones to supportive ones. After working through some examples together, the parents can try to repeat the exercise on their own, and the therapist can gauge their ability to make this distinction and formulate supportive statements.

SUPPORT IS DIFFERENT FROM DEMAND

Supportive responses also differ from demanding ones. A demanding parent expects their child to act and feel differently than they do. For example, a parent who responds to their anxious child with statements such as "Get over it," "Cut it out," or even just "Don't worry about it" are suggesting the child should be better able to decide how to feel. This not only unnecessarily minimizes the challenge facing the child (and thus does not express acceptance and is not supportive), it also is likely to leave a child feeling misunderstood or frustrated at not being able to meet the parent's expectation. Children with anxiety disorders cannot simply choose not to feel anxious and suggesting they should be able to is not supportive.

Parents may find this confusing as well. After all, isn't part of support the confidence in the child's ability to cope? How is a parent to express this confidence without suggesting the child should feel differently? Replacing accommodation with support solves this challenge at two levels. First, the confidence expressed in supportive responses focuses on the child's ability to tolerate anxiety, not the ability to not feel it. A parent is not saying, "I know you can feel less anxious." Rather, in being supportive they are saying, "I know you are able to tolerate some anxiety." Second, by reducing accommodation, the parent is shifting the focus away from what the child does and focusing instead on what they themselves do as parents. In other words, the parent is not saying to the child "I know you can cope so you have to do this." Rather, they are saying "I know you can cope, and so I'm going to do this." Or in some cases, "I know you can cope, and so I'm *not* going to do this."

This emphasis on parental behavior rather than child behavior is one of the more powerful tools in the clinician's toolbox when working with parents of anxious children. Parents and therapists usually—sometimes even exclusively—tend to focus on the child's behavior. This is to be expected as the child is the one with the anxiety disorder and the one whose difficulties are being treated in therapy. And yet, accommodation is a parental behavior. It is engendered by the child's anxiety, but, ultimately, it is the parents who are either accommodating or not.

When working with parents, succumbing to the tendency to focus on the child's behavior is usually counterproductive. Parents are not actually able to dictate the pace at which a child will progress in overcoming the anxiety disorder, and so a therapist whose guidance to parents is focused on the child's behavior is often placing them in an untenable situation. To comply with the therapist's guidance, they must ensure that the child behaves a certain way, but they have no actual means of ensuring that she will. All too frequently, trying to comply with such guidance will lead parents to try to compel the child, and the result can be an escalation in parent–child conflict. The acknowledgement and validation that are crucial ingredients of support are soon forgotten when parents try to force a behavioral change on a reluctant child. This kind of forceful and escalatory dynamic can be completely avoided by ensuring that the goal of the parent work is not to directly modify the child's behavior at all. Rather, the parental goal can be either to simply express support for the child in the earlier stages of treatment or to place in supportive context the change in their own behavior, once a plan for reduced accommodation has been developed. Developing plans for reducing accommodation is the topic of the next chapter.

ROLE PLAY

Role-playing and practicing with parents the supportive responses they will provide to their anxious child can help to ensure that they have understood the therapist's message and increases the likelihood that they will deliver the supportive message as planned. Even a parent who has well understood the notion of supportive statements and is able to make supportive statements in the session may falter under the stress of dealing with an anxious child or a barrage of anxiety symptoms. Stress can impede memory and cognitive faculties, and many parents will remember only after the interaction is over that they had planned to react in a different manner. Role play can help to overcome this problem and reduces the likelihood that the parent will revert to accommodating their child.

During the role play, the therapist will strive to act the part of the anxious child as convincingly as possible. Asking parents how the anxious child usually behaves can help with this. For example, is the child prone to whining? Are they tearful? Do they get angry or loud? The more realistically the therapist can portray the child's behavior and bring the scene to life, the better prepared the parent will be. Another strategy is to ask the parent to act the part of the child first, with the therapist playing the role of the supportive parent. Again, the therapist should encourage the parent not to hold back and to deliver as convincing a portrayal of their child's behavior as possible. This strategy has the additional benefit of allowing the therapist to model for the parent what a supportive response would look and sound like. The parent can then play their own part after watching the therapist do it first.

> *OK, let's practice what we've been talking about. Imagine you're at home. It's 7:30, and you're trying to get Natalee to bed. We know she's probably going to be begging you to stay with her and telling you she can't be in the room on her own. Let's practice that supportive response we just talked about. Remember, support is acceptance and confidence together. How about I do it first, and you be Natalee? OK? You're going to be a very scared little Natalee who's never spent a night on her own as long as she can remember, right? Now, don't go easy on me. I want you to make it just as difficult for me as you think Natalee might make it for you tonight. My job is going to be to react in that supportive manner. Do you think Natalee is going to hear you make a supportive statement and right away feel all calm and happy? Right, so don't do that either. Just try to act like her and let's see if I can take it.*
>
> *[. . .]*
>
> *OK, that was hard wasn't it! It sure helped me understand what you're dealing with. Now let's flip it around. I'll try to be Natalee, and you be the supportive parent. This is your chance to practice so that tonight you'll be a natural. I'll take my cues from what you did when you were playing Natalee. Ready? OK, here goes . . .*

Parents may feel that their words sound awkward or feel artificial when they first begin to practice implementing supportive statements. In a sense, this is almost inevitable. Artificial is an opposite of natural, and the therapist is asking them to behave in a manner that is different from what comes naturally. All parents have some natural responses that have become instilled through repetition and habit.

When parents voice this concern, it may be best to acknowledge that, indeed, any change in habit is likely to feel artificial at first. But the therapist can also remind the parent that artificial does not mean bad; it merely denotes a change that has not yet become ingrained. And with practice and repetition, the supportive statements can come to feel just as natural as their previous response. Importantly, the supportive statements do not need to feel natural to have a positive impact on the child. Likewise, the therapist can suggest that since the previous responses did not lead to the desired outcome, it makes sense to try something new. Engaging the parents in formulating the supportive statements, using their own words rather than the therapist's, will help the statements feel less forced or rehearsed. In the exchange between Kristen and her therapist earlier in this chapter, Kristen was able to come up with a supportive statement for her son Ian that was different from one the therapist might have suggested. By embracing this statement and praising Kristen for thinking of it, the therapist made it more likely that Kristen would remember and use the supportive statement and that it would feel like something that is truly "hers."

8

Planning How Parents Will Reduce Accommodation

Formulating a well-thought-out plan for the changes the parents will make to their accommodating behavior is among the most important things the therapist will do in addressing family accommodation. A hastily devised plan, or one that is not specific and detailed enough, or that does not take into consideration the challenges it will pose for the parents in its actual implementation, is likely to fail. When this happens, the parents' confidence in themselves and in the therapist can be shaken, and they may be less likely to make additional efforts or persist with a future plan. Of course, no therapist can predict every eventuality that the parents will encounter. It is not necessary to do so, and even a very well thought out plan may have to be revised and modified in light of new information or additional experience. But investing time in crafting as good a plan as possible with the information currently available is worthwhile. This chapter highlights some considerations for the therapist in devising accommodation reduction plans.

BE SPECIFIC AND DETAILED

A good plan will describe in detail exactly which accommodations are going to be changed, the specific situations in which the changes will be implemented, and the degree of change the parents will implement. For example, if parents have been accommodating by arriving very early to events due to generalized anxiety, the plan can specify which events will now not be arrived at early and which events will continue to be accommodated as they were previously. The plan can also state exactly how much later they will arrive to the targeted events. Will they arrive exactly on time, or will they arrive less early than before? In fact, because it is very difficult for anyone to predict precisely when they will arrive anywhere, the plan may be more practical if it focuses on when the parents and child leave the house rather than when they arrive at the event. The plan would also have to describe how parents will respond when the child is anxiously prompting them to leave at the usual time. Will they ignore the child's prodding? Will they respond with a supportive statement? How many pleas will they reply to before perhaps ignoring additional requests?

To take another example, if parents have been accommodating a socially anxious child by not inviting guests to the home, the plan can specify how many guests will now come over, who those guests will be, and the frequency of the visits. The therapist and parents can discuss the degree of preparation that guests need to receive in advance of visiting the home. Should they be asked to address the child or to leave them be? How should they respond if the child does not reply, or if the child behaves in an inappropriate manner because they are anxious or angry about the visit? Should the child be informed in advance of each and every visit, or should they only be told that guests will be visiting? How should parents respond if the child chooses to avoid the guests altogether, for example, by staying in their room or leaving the house? Each of these questions, if not discussed as part of the plan, opens the door for parental responses that are less deliberate and more impulsive. A parent who is embarrassed by a child who ignores a guest and seems to be behaving rudely, for example, may feel pressured to engage in unhelpful escalation, trying to force the child to be polite or to discipline them for not acting as they expect.

In another example, consider a parent who has accommodated by answering repeated phone calls during times of separation. The parent will a require a detailed plan that addresses when exactly they will not respond to the phone calls and how many calls, if any, they will still agree to take. A therapist working with parents in this situation may also need to address the question of whether parents will worry that the child has an actual emergency that requires their attention. Otherwise, the parents may ultimately feel that not answering the phone poses too high a risk and not be able to put the plan into practice.

By considering as many details as possible and devising a plan that is highly specific, the therapist is increasing the likelihood that the plan will stand up to the pressures of reality. Vagueness and ambiguity in the accommodation reduction plan are counterproductive and can increase the likelihood of disagreement or conflict between the two parents, as each of them may have a different understanding of how the plan should be executed. For example, if a plan calls for the parents to refrain from speaking for the child in public, one parent may assume that the parents should be initiating situations in which this would normally occur, while the other parent may see this as heavy-handed and assume that the plan should only be implemented when the opportunity presents itself spontaneously. Both interpretations are plausible, but in the absence of clear guidance from the therapist, the opposing views can lead to argument and mutual frustration. Disagreement between the parents can also cause parents to delay implementing the plan at all until the next session (at which time they can clarify the therapist' intent) and to be less enthusiastic about a process that has already led to strife between them.

CONSISTENCY

As with all behavior modification plans, consistency is key to success. Parents who are consistent and persistent in the execution of the accommodation reduction plan will facilitate a faster adjustment both for themselves and their child. The plan should, therefore, address any situations that will make it harder for parents to act in a consistent manner. It is useful to remember that a consistent plan does not necessarily mean that parents always behave a certain way—only that they consistently execute the plan as prescribed. By analogy, a patient may be prescribed a medication to be taken every two days. Consistent adherence to this prescription does not mean taking the medication every day! It means only that the patient will, in fact, take the medication every two days and not deviate from this plan. Likewise, there may be good reason for parents to plan to reduce their accommodation in one setting but not in another. And consistent execution of this plan does not mean trying to modify their behavior in all settings (which would, in fact, not be adherence to the plan at all). Rather, consistent execution of the plan means only that they will always reduce the accommodation in the agreed-upon situations. A plan that targets only some situations but that a parent feels confident about is preferable to a more global plan that the parent does not feel is reasonable or has doubts about.

Acting in a consistent manner will make it easier for the child to predict the parental behavior, with the benefit being speedier acclimation to the new behavior and shorter "extinction bursts" as the child adjusts. The therapist can remind parents that "anxiety and unpredictability are not friends," that anxious children tend to respond negatively to the loss of control that comes with not being able to predict what will occur. Since the objective of the plan is to encourage better independent coping and reduce anxiety, a consistent and predictable plan is likely to work best.

Cayden was eight years old and had separation anxiety. Cayden would become extremely tearful and whiny at even the briefest separation and would physically cling to his parents many times throughout the day, even when they were only leaving a room. His mother Susan was particularly frustrated about Cayden's behavior when she would try to shower. If Susan took a shower when her husband Jeff was not home, Cayden would knock constantly on the bathroom door and insist that she answer him many times. Susan felt that the imposition on her shower time was robbing her of her one relaxing time in the day. Susan and Jeff planned that each afternoon or evening, Jeff would go out to run an errand or take Cayden's baby sister for a stroll, and Susan would take a shower. They informed Cayden of the plan, and Susan told him she would not be answering him while she was in the shower but that she would play a game with him when she came out.

After the first week, Susan reported that the plan had not gone well. When Jeff left the house and Susan told Cayden that she was going to take a shower, Cayden immediately started to cry and clung to Susan begging her not to shower. Susan was overwrought and found it hard to cope with Cayden's obvious distress. She managed to make a supportive statement and to detach Cayden from her and "bolted" into the bathroom. Cayden knocked on the door and called to her plaintively. When she did not respond, Cayden began pounding on the door and crying loudly. Unable to tolerate it, Susan ultimately answered as usual. The following day Susan dreaded repeating the experience and devised a modified plan instead. Rather than having Jeff leave the house, he would be in his study with the door closed while she showered. The scene from the previous day repeated itself, and Susan ended up feeling more exhausted than ever. On the third day, Susan again tried a modification to the plan. This time she would shower earlier in the day, before Jeff came home. Susan hoped that by trying different things she would hit upon a solution that allowed her to shower without Cayden becoming so agitated. Each day, Susan tried another solution, but none of them worked. The best day, she told the therapist, was when Cayden was engrossed in watching a favorite YouTube video and she "snuck out of the room and showered." Cayden only noticed what was happening when she was almost done with her quicker-than-usual shower. All in all, Susan felt that, with the exception of that one day, the plan had not gone well, and Cayden's anxiety did not seem any better.

The therapist in this example noted several things that appeared to be happening. Susan clearly hoped that she could find a way to reduce her accommodation without triggering anxiety in Cayden. His dramatic expressions of distress were very difficult for her, and Susan was clearly not yet prepared to tolerate them. In essence, Susan was trying to find a shortcut. Rather than allowing Cayden to learn that his anxiety would subside if not accommodated, Susan wished that he could not experience it at all. Her repeated attempts at modifying the plan reflected her hope that with enough creativity she may stumble upon the "right" solution— one that would allow her to shower in peace and have Cayden not become upset. Describing the day on which she showered while Cayden was distracted by the video as "the best day" confirms that in Susan's mind, a successful implementation of the plan is one in which Cayden does not become upset, rather than one in which she reduces the accommodation and Cayden copes with the anxiety.

But Susan's creativity was also having another important effect. By changing the plan every day, Susan was making the shower experience extremely unpredictable from Cayden's point of view. Because every day was a little different, Cayden had no way of knowing when Susan was going to shower. Even her "sneaking" off to the shower while Cayden was watching YouTube, while successful in her view, likely led to more anxiety and vigilance on Cayden's part. It is likely that if Susan had felt more able to tolerate Cayden's anxiety and had implemented the same plan in a predictable manner for several days in a row (without answering him while she was showering), Cayden would have become used to this and discovered that he could handle the situation better than either of them thought possible. But this could not occur because of the constant changes and modifications.

The therapist tried to explain this to the parents with a metaphor:

Imagine that Cayden was sick and had to get a shot every day. Not terribly painful but definitely unpleasant. Which do you think would go better: If every day, at around 4:00 PM you gave Cayden his shot even if he became fussy or upset or if you tried to find some way to give him his shot without his objecting and you tried something new every day. One day you might do it at 4:00. But he cried, so the next day you waited until he was going to sleep and then gave it to him. But he didn't like that either so the next day you woke him up and, immediately, it was shot time. But that also didn't go well, so the next day you hid behind the sofa and suddenly popped out with the shot. Or maybe one day you try to just give it to him without him noticing by doing it in the middle of a conversation or in the car or you arrive at school and do it during recess. It seems like this would be pretty confusing to Cayden, doesn't it? He would find it hard to ever relax because who knows, maybe a shot is coming, right? You'd be trying so hard to avoid him getting upset but he would just be getting worse and worse. Wouldn't it be easier to just know that there's this one moment in the day, predictable and expected, like clockwork, when he gets his shot? And then he'd know that he's done with it for the day. He'd probably get used to that much faster, right? Because it's easier to get used to something that's predictable than to something unpredictable. It's the same with the shower. If we keep surprising Cayden and changing the rules, he doesn't get much chance to learn the rules. In fact, there are no rules for him to learn.

STRESS TEST THE PLAN

A useful way to improve and strengthen a plan for reducing accommodation is to "stress test" it, by trying to think together with the parents about all the ways in which the plan might fail. Are there going to be situations in which the parents will be less able to execute the plan? Can they think about possible consequences that would be intolerable to them? Will there be circumstances when they won't have time to deal with a child's insistence on accommodation? Or when it will be too awkward or embarrassing? Assuming that parents will be able to maintain their resolve under all circumstances is unrealistic and sets the stage for inconsistency or failure. The therapist can encourage the parents to be as candid as possible. "Tell me why this is not going to work" is an open invitation that encourages parents to share any misgivings that they may have but feel it is impolite or inappropriate to express. For example, if parents are planning to reduce their accommodation by not agreeing to leave public places when a child begins to experience panic symptoms, they may need to consider what to do if the child creates a disturbance that interferes with others in a public setting. Or if parents resolve not to accommodate by picking a child up early from school, they will have to also plan for how to respond if they get a call from the school when the child is anxious. Later chapters offer some helpful solutions for troubleshooting common challenges in implementing plans for reducing accommodation. Subjecting the plan to this kind of stress test can help to preempt many of those challenges and facilitate a better process by considering the solutions in advance.

KEEP THE FOCUS ON THE PARENTS

The plan for changes to parents' accommodation should be carefully constructed to maintain the focus on the parents' behavior and not be contingent on the child behaving in a certain way. That is to say, the plan should explicitly focus on what the parents will or will not do. This is doubly important when the parent work is not being done in conjunction with child therapy or when the degree of coordination with the child's own therapy is low. However, even when devised together with the child, the plan should still maintain its focus on the parents' behavior. For example, in a case of selective mutism, a child might agree to a plan that specifies that the parents will not speak in place of them when going out to eat. But the plan remains parent-focused and does not require that the child speak for themselves. A therapist and child might collaboratively craft a plan for him to order for himself, as a step on an exposure hierarchy, but the child's plan is best kept separate and distinct from the parents' plan not to accommodate by speaking for him.

Maintaining the focus of the plan on parental behavior serves dual purposes. First, it reduces the likelihood of parents trying to exert unhelpful pressure on the child to comply. Even a child who has agreed in the therapist's office to order for himself might quail in the moment and refuse to speak. If parents are clear that their goal is only to refrain from the accommodating behavior, there will be less pressure on them to try to prod the child into speaking, a behavior that is likely to backfire and make the child less compliant in the future. In fact, when a child has agreed to the plan, it becomes even more important that parents understand their plan relates only to their own behavior. Parents of a child who has consented to a plan in therapy can feel frustrated if the child "breaks their word" by not complying in the actual moment. Or they might feel that the child is leading the therapist astray or wasting resources expended on therapy by not following through. Cognitive-behavioral therapists are used to children not always succeeding in every exposure they undertake, and these setbacks are taken in stride. Parents, on the other hand, may be more likely to demonstrate exasperation or pressure when disappointed by setbacks.

The second benefit of maintaining focus on the parents' behavior is a clearer definition of what constitutes successful implementation of the plan. If the parents believe that the plan calls for a particular behavior in their child, then they will only consider it successful if the child acts as expected. In contrast, if the plan is entirely focused on the parents' behavior, then its success is also based only on their behavior. To return to the example of the child with selective mutism, if the parents believe that the plan is for the child to speak for himself, then they will not feel they have succeeded unless he does so. Whereas if the parents understand that the plan called only for them not to accommodate, then success for the current step is defined only as them not having spoken for him. Change in child behavior is the long-term goal of the intervention, not the immediate objective. Often, even when the therapist has clearly articulated the focus on the parents' behavior, parents are initially disappointed that an immediate change in child behavior has not occurred. This reflects their underlying hope for rapid improvement in the child's anxiety and affords the therapist an opportunity to reiterate the big picture, return the focus to what the parents did or did not do, and reframe a perceived defeat into a resounding triumph.

Tara had difficulty being away from her parents and particularly struggled with extracurricular activities. She had been going to gymnastics for over a year but refused to stay unless one of her parents stayed with her. Her father, Bubin, had managed with difficulty to reach the point where he would sit at the side of the classroom instead of right next to her, but that was the extent of the progress. Staying with Tara at gymnastics was inconvenient, but Tara enjoyed the class, and both parents believed it was helpful to her physical development. In working with the therapist, Bubin agreed to drop Tara off at gymnastics and then to leave and go wait in the car until the class was over. He spoke with Tara's gymnastics teacher ahead of time and arranged for the teacher to meet them outside before the class and take Tara by the hand so that Bubin could leave.

When they arrived at the gym, Bubin handed Tara over to the teacher and swiftly made his departure to go wait in the car. Halfway through the class, feeling curious and a little nervous about how things were going, Bubin got out of the car and went around the side of the building to look in the window. He saw Tara sitting in the doorway, looking a little teary and not participating in any activities. When he came back to pick her up at the end of class, the teacher confirmed she had sat there the whole time, not doing any of the exercises or interacting with other children. Bubin was disappointed and started the next session with the therapist saying, "Thumbs down."

The therapist reminded Bubin that the plan had not been "You'll drop Tara off, wait in the car, and she'll feel good and have a regular gymnastics class" but rather "You'll drop Tara off and wait in the car until the class is over." The therapist was empathetic about Bubin's hope that things would have gone better for Tara but explained that this may be premature: "Look, every time Tara goes to the gym, she's practicing physical gymnastics. But this time it's like she was doing two classes at once: She had regular gymnastics, like jumping or backflips, but she also had emotional gymnastics, being away from you. Think about the first time she went, could she do everything she does now? Probably not, right? It took time and practice for her to get good at physical gymnastics, and it takes time to get good at emotional gymnastics as well. She can't be a medalist on her first try! This was a great first time. She didn't run out after you, and she didn't spend the whole time crying. When you peeked in half way through she was teary, but she already stopped crying. That's great progress. And the main thing is, you did it! You left her, you waited until the end, you got her, and she survived! Doing something one time doesn't make it easy. It just proves that it's possible. That's something she knows now that she didn't know before—that she can get through a whole class without you being there and still be OK. That's huge. And that's something you gave her this week that she never had before. Let's give her time to get good at emotional gymnastics before we start handing out the scores, OK?"'

Maintaining the focus on the parents' behavior and reframing experiences such as Bubin's from failure to success has another important implication: It allows the parent to reflect that success back to the child. A parent like Bubin, who is disappointed that their child did not respond to the reduced accommodation as they had hoped, will also find it difficult to praise the child for what they see as a defeat. But by focusing on whether or not the parent accommodated rather than on what the child did or did not do, it becomes easier to acknowledge that the child has coped with something new, regardless of how they responded to it. Tara herself may have been feeling disappointed with her gymnastics class, which she usually enjoyed, and likely was able to detect her father's disappointment as well. Her experience may have been different if Bubin had picked her up with a hug and told her how proud he felt that she had got through something so hard. Chapter 7 emphasized that in expressing support, parents are not conveying their confidence that the child will necessarily do a certain thing, but rather their confidence that their child is able to tolerate anxiety related distress. In much the same way, a plan that focuses on parent change rather than child change allows parents to express their pride in a child's accomplishment at having tolerated the anxiety, regardless of how the child behaved in actual fact. This is another example of the power of focusing on parent behavior. Parents can essentially "impose success" on a child simply by deciding to act a certain way and adhering to that plan. Indeed, the more resistance a child displayed to the parental behavior or the more difficulty they experienced as a result of it, the more a therapist may want to emphasize the child's accomplishment and encourage the parents to do so as well by lavishing praise on the child. A child who fears they have disappointed their parent or angered them by not responding better is likely to be defensive and resistant in subsequent situations. The therapist can help them to disarm the child's defensiveness and make the next time easier rather than harder, by surprising them with praise instead of reproach.

COMMUNICATING THE PLAN TO THE CHILD

When addressing family accommodation, whether through work with parents alone or conjunction with child therapy, open and transparent communication with the child is essential. Communicating plans to the child prior to implementing changes in parental behavior can be achieved either through direct therapist–child conversations or by guiding the parent to deliver a supportive and clear message to the child.

In many families, the topic of accommodation will have become almost taboo, something that is rarely discussed. And when it is addressed, the discussions may have taken on a negative, conflictual, or otherwise aversive nature for both parents and children. Parents' frustration with the burden that accommodation has imposed on them, their exasperation or simmering anger at the child for the disruption to family life, and the child's discomfort or embarrassment at needing the accommodations can contribute to an enduring avoidance of the topic. Prior conversations have often not been fruitful. In the absence of effective therapeutic guidance, parents' sporadic attempts to talk with the child about accommodation have frequently backfired, culminating in argument or heated altercation. If a child has been using forceful means to impose accommodation on parents or siblings, such as physical or verbal aggression, the conversation may have been more disciplinary than supportive in nature. This tendency, toward scolding and argument, may have been exacerbated by parents' natural predisposition to tackle the issue of accommodation mainly when feeling most frustrated about it. For example, if a parent has had to make a change to a plan, missed an important event, or just spent a sleepless night accommodating their child, they may be motivated to make it clear to the child that the situation is unacceptable and cannot go on. But these are also the moments when their ability to articulate their perspective in a supportive manner is likely to be at its weakest. The child is also likely to be less receptive in such moments. Feeling guilty about their difficulty (and equally tired from the lack of sleep), the child is more prone to respond in a negative manner, making it harder for the parent to get through to them and pushing the conversation in less fruitful directions.

Ask about Previous Communication

Before providing guidance on how to talk to the child about the accommodation, the therapist may want to ask parents (and children, when possible) about times in the past when they have confronted the issue.

- *When was the last time you talked with your child about these accommodations? How did that conversation go?*
- *Are you afraid of how your child will react if you raise this topic?*
- *Does your child ever bring it up? How do you respond?*
- *Who usually talks with them about it?*
- *What did you say?*
- *What did the child say?*
- *Do you think your child knows how you feel? Do they understand how much this is affecting you?*
- *Do any of your other children ever tell them anything about the accommodation?*
- *Has anyone outside of the immediate family ever talked with your child about this? Who was it? What did they say? How did your child react?*

Asking about previous discussions will provide the therapist information helpful in shaping effective communication. If parents have generally scolded the child, it may be important to spend time coaching them on a different style of communication and role-playing how they will act differently now. If parents are worried about the child's responses at the topic of accommodation, it can be useful to help them prepare by choosing a time and place when the child is least likely to react explosively. Or, if parents have a style of communication characterized by high affect, it may be helpful to coach them on being more matter of fact and less emotional. High levels of affect are usually counterproductive in discussing accommodation, regardless of the specific emotion being addressed. Becoming angry is particularly unhelpful, but even parents who become very sad when talking about their child's difficulty and have difficulty containing their emotion will have a hard time leading a fruitful conversation. Likewise, parents overwhelmed with compassion for the child or whose discouragement and frustration permeates their communication will struggle to engage the child. And, of course, parents who appear to be ridiculing the child for what they perceive as irrational behavior will have a hard time being supportive.

Hearing about the child's previous reactions can also help the therapist coach the parents in preparation for raising the issue of family accommodation. If a child generally tries to avoid the issue by changing the topic, leaving the room, refusing to answer, or taking other evasive measures, parents can prepare for this by crafting brief unilateral statements that they can make swiftly without demanding a response from the child. Sometimes creating a written message, delivered to the child physically or electronically can take the place of verbal communication. Likewise, a child who is prone to outbursts, "counterattacks," or externalizing symptoms may do better if the parents deliver concise and supportive communication. Having another person from outside the immediate family circle present when the parents address the accommodation can cause some discomfort but can help to reduce the likelihood of overly reactive responses.

Be Supportive

The therapist can help ensure that the parents address the accommodation and communicate their plan to the child in a supportive manner by reviewing with them what they will say and suggesting adjustments. If parents omit an acknowledgement of the child's genuine distress, for example, the therapist can suggest starting with a statement that explicitly recognizes the child's anxiety and the distress that their reduced accommodation may cause. Or, if parents focus only on the change they will make and do not express confidence in the child's ability to cope with and tolerate distress, the therapist can suggest appending a statement that clearly conveys this element of support. When the message is to be written, rather than spoken, the therapist can review the text before it is delivered and suggest modifications as needed.

Box 8.1

Developing a Plan for Reducing Accommodation

- *Be specific and detailed*—A vague plan is less likely to be implemented consistently and requires parents to improvise.
- *Stress test the plan*—Think about and talk over the challenges the parents will face in implementing the plan.
- *Be consistent*—Strive for consistency but, remember, consistent does not mean *always*!
- *Keep the focus on the parents*—Check to make sure the plan involves only changes to parent behavior—not child behavior!
- *Communicate the plan to the child*—If parents will inform the child, role-play presenting the plan in a supportive manner.

Be Specific

Clear and specific information about the changes parents plan to implement is preferable to more vague or ambiguous statements that can leave the child wondering what exactly parents are going to do. Anxious children will likely respond with even more anxiety in the face of vague or ill-defined plans. Anxiety tends to heighten children's need to feel in control, a sensation that stems from being able to predict and impact future events. While parents acting to reduce their accommodation may be reducing the child's control by electing to change their behavior without the child's consent, there is no need to further diminish the child's control by also making those changes unpredictable. On the contrary, providing the child with knowledge about the changes that will occur will help to maintain a feeling of control and lower both the anxiety and the resistance to the plan. Parents who fear that their child will react negatively to the plan they have made will sometimes prefer to avoid confrontation by not communicating the actual plan to the child and omitting its specific details from the conversation. But this avoidance will likely engender only more confrontation, as the child becomes more and more anxious about what is to come and persists in asking questions that the parents are trying to avoid. Ultimately, they are likely to be worn down by these questions, but at this point the information is provided unwillingly and with more negative emotion than had they clearly stated their intent from the beginning. Hiding from the child what they intend to do can also increase the child's sense that parents are acting harmfully or against them, leading to more resentment or resistance. For all these reasons, the therapist will usually help parents the most if they encourage clear, specific, and detailed communication of the accommodation reduction plan (see Box 8.1).

9

Obstacles to Addressing Accommodation

Addressing family accommodation in treating childhood anxiety can be a challenging process requiring flexibility, creativity, and, oftentimes, a deft touch of diplomacy. Some of the challenges that therapists encounter are challenges that can arise in any therapeutic work with parents. Others are challenges that are more specific to the goal of addressing accommodation of child anxiety. This chapter addresses some of the common challenges and pitfalls in addressing family accommodation and provides practical solutions for overcoming them. An exhaustive list of all the possible difficulties would be impossible, but the challenges discussed in this chapter are among the most common, and the solutions provided are those that have proven themselves effective and useful over the accumulated experience of working with many children and families.

CHALLENGES IN COOPERATION BETWEEN PARENTS

As any therapist who has worked with parents knows, achieving a productive and harmonious working alliance between two parents is never taken for granted. Many things can make such a collaborative alliance challenging. For example, parents may disagree on how best to approach or even define the problem. Frequently, they are meeting with the therapist only at the insistence of one of the parents and perhaps even over the objections of the other. Parents also have genuinely different experiences with the child. They will typically spend different amounts of time with the child, doing different things, and observe different behavioral patterns in the child. And children do not behave in the same manner with each of their parents, further increasing the likelihood that parental perceptions will differ meaningfully. In some cases, parents will bring an accumulation of feelings of blame, resentment, or criticism to the therapy sessions. It is not uncommon for parents to attribute the child's problems to the behavior of a spouse, leading to frustration on the side of the parent attributing blame and to resentment or indignation on the part of the parent being faulted. Even marital conflict that is not directly related to the child's anxiety problem will present a barrier. It is easy for the parent work to become one more arena in which old battles play out, and familiar arguments between parents are rehashed. It is incumbent on the therapist to identify obstacles to parental cooperation and to address these in a way that promotes the couple's ability to effectively modify their accommodating behavior.

In working with many families of anxious children, one of the most common dynamics observed between parents is that of one parent providing ever-increasing levels of accommodation, while the other parent refuses to accommodate and places unrealistic demands for better coping and functioning on the part of the child. In this common scenario, both parents are likely to begin working with the therapist with mutual feelings of resentment and blame. The accommodating parent views their partner as overly harsh or demanding, while the more demanding parent views the other as weak and as an obstacle to the child's functioning.

The therapist can address this situation by reminding parents that their goal is ultimately the same—to help their child be less anxious and function better. While the strategies preferred by each parent differ, acknowledging that they both are striving towards the same goal can help to reduce some of the blame and accusations. But the therapist can further advance the working alliance by returning to the notion of "support" described throughout this book. Support in the context of an anxious child can be defined as the integration of two messages: a message of acceptance and validation for the difficulty the child is experiencing and a message of confidence in the child's ability to tolerate distress and to cope even without accommodation. The therapist can point out to the parents that they are each, in fact, representing one of the crucial elements of support. The more demanding parent is conveying to the child the belief in their ability to cope, while the more accommodating parent is expressing a recognition of the child's distress. By formulating the parents' opposing behaviors as two components of the supportive message, rather than as conflicting messages that interfere with each other, the therapist can reduce the conflict between parents and promote more effective collaboration. Framing the parental behaviors in this way also helps the therapist to avoid being perceived as aligned with only one of the parents, a perception that increases the risk of alienating the other parent.

In some cases, both parents express agreement with the therapist's suggestions during the session, but one parent consistently fails to implement the suggested steps while the other does so frequently. This pattern will often frustrate both the therapist and the more compliant parent, and both may begin to lose faith in the therapeutic process. One way to salvage the situation is for the therapist to identify the barriers facing the less compliant parent, which may be easier to do during a private conversation with that parent alone. It may be that the parent has been reluctant to express a difference of opinion during the sessions, or that they struggle emotionally with the child's distress, or that they have not fully understood the plan. Creating a nonjudgmental context in which to explore what is hampering the parent's execution of the plan is key to solving the problem.

In other situations, however, the most effective strategy may be to accept that at this particular point in time this parent is not able to implement the therapist's suggestions. This need not mean that the process cannot continue effectively or even that the less compliant parent cannot contribute meaningfully to its success. Accepting the limitations of what the parent is able to do at a given time can actually help advance the process by reducing the frustration that stems from what is factually an unrealistic expectation. Since the parent is expressing agreement during the session, it can be understood that they do not object in principle to the plan and are merely not able to execute it themselves. They may be better able to take on other helpful roles, including supporting their spouse who is better suited to the actual behavioral changes. Reducing the accommodation of one parent in a consistent fashion is still a meaningful change for the child and one that is likely to help in treating their anxiety. As the process continues, the parent, now freed from their "noncompliant" status, may observe their child coping with the change and feel more able to follow suit in their own behavior as well.

DEALING WITH CHILD AGGRESSION

Anxiety and externalizing problems are often comorbid, and many anxious children will also exhibit behavioral problems including rage, physical aggression, verbal aggression, or destructive behaviors directed toward objects or property. Even children who do not have a history of aggressive behavior may react with anger, irritability, or aggression to their parents choosing to reduce accommodation. Some parents will fear this possibility, and their apprehension may make it more difficult for them to follow through on plans to reduce accommodation. Other parents may feel surprised or alarmed by their child's aggression and wonder if reducing accommodation is making things worse. Providing parents with a framework for understanding the child's behavior and tools for coping with possible aggression can help overcome both possibilities. A helpful process for addressing such behaviors includes four components: (a) understanding where the aggression is "coming from" and what it means; (b) avoiding escalation of the aggression; (c) determining whether any response is needed; and (d) nonescalating means of responding when necessary. Each of these steps is discussed next in more detail.

Understanding the Aggression

Emphasizing a few key points to parents will help them understand their child's aggressive reactions to reduced accommodation. First, it is useful to acknowledge that by reducing their accommodating behavior, parents are the ones taking the initiative to "break the rules" that have been in place. By providing accommodation in the past, parents have made it a reasonable expectation on the part of the child that they will continue to do so in the future as well. And so, reducing accommodation even when preceded by explanations and supportive communication on the part of the parents can often take a child by surprise. When the parent work is being done without child involvement, this is even more likely to be the case, as the child will not have had the opportunity to discuss the plan in a therapy session. Reducing the accommodation is valuable and will help the child over time, but in the immediate term, it may well feel to the child like a violation of an unspoken agreement and can be both confusing and anxiety-provoking. It is not surprising that some children would respond to this with anger.

Second, it is useful to remember that an anxious child can feel as though their parent accommodating is the only way for them to escape distressing feelings of anxiety. Over time, the child will learn that this is not the case and that they are able to regulate their own anxiety and to calm themselves. But at the start of the process, the child does not know or believe this. The parents' refusal to accommodate can be seen by the child as blocking their only path to feeling calm again or to being able to function without anxiety. It is not surprising that some children would respond to this with anger as well. Accepting that this is the child's experience can help to reduce parental escalation when faced with a child who is behaving aggressively.

Third, the therapist can remind the parents that anger and aggression are part of the anxiety response, part of "flight or fight." Viewing the child's aggression as a manifestation of anxiety, rather than as merely being inappropriate or unacceptable, can increase their empathy and reduce anger.

Taking all three points together, the therapist can help the parents remain calm and feel less of a need to discipline a child who is reacting aggressively to reduced accommodation. Rather than seeing their child as misbehaving, the parents will be better able to see the child as anxious and upset and to acknowledge their own responsibility in triggering these feelings. A useful analogy may be the behavior of a child who is terrified of needles and lashes out when faced with getting a shot. It is both unhelpful and unfair to get very angry at this child for the manifestation of their panic or terror. But it is human for parents to react with anger, nonetheless. Remembering that the child is simply scared can help parents remain calm and empathic. In much the same way, it does not make good sense to become very angry at a child for responding with anger to the parental decision to withhold accommodation. Remembering that the child is feeling very scared can help parents remain calm.

Avoiding Escalation of the Aggression

Faced with a child who is acting aggressively, many parents will feel pressure to respond to the child's behavior, either through discipline or surrender to accommodation. Both of these responses are ultimately unhelpful and actually increase the likelihood of more aggressive behavior in the future. Attempting to discipline a child who is scared and confused and lashing out is not effective and will usually drive the child to further increase their own aggression in a cycle of escalation.

Conversely, giving in to the aggression and returning to the accommodation reinforces the behavior and establishes aggression as a means of achieving the child's goals.

Often the best response to a child behaving aggressively because of reduced accommodation is no response at all. Of course, if a child is acting in a way that is dangerous to themselves or to another person, the parents will have to take action to prevent that danger, but their intervention can be limited to this goal only, rather than also trying to "teach the child a lesson," reprimand them, or convey their displeasure with the behavior. If, indeed, a parental response is needed at all, it can come later after the child and the parents are calm. In many cases, however, once having calmed down, parents will realize that there is no actual need for a response. Simply continuing the plan to reduce accommodation, while acknowledging difficulty for the child, may be all the support that is needed.

Avoiding escalation can be difficult, however. Even the most serene parent can be pushed to the limit when faced with a child who is acting out. The therapist can recommend to the parents that they try to avoid the situation altogether. When no safety threat is present, parents can simply walk away and trust that the child will eventually calm down and, in fact, will calm sooner than if the parents stayed actively trying to soothe them.

Determine If Any Response Is Needed

As previously noted, "in the moment" while a child is reacting aggressively to reduced accommodation there is little point in any response apart from what is necessary to prevent immediate danger. Once calm has been restored, parents can decide whether the child's behavior requires an additional response or not. The therapist can be helpful in this decision, and it is often worth postponing any response until after the parents have an opportunity to discuss the issue with the therapist. Even when parents feel strongly that the behavior was not acceptable and loathe to allow it to pass without additional attention, it is worthwhile to discuss and consider the disadvantages of potential parental responses. In particular, by focusing on the aggressive behavior, parents are allowing the child to shift the focus of their efforts away from reducing accommodation and toward reduction in aggressive behavior. This is usually undesirable. In the case of a child who has often behaved aggressively in the past, it seems pointless to choose this particular time, when the focus is on the anxiety, to also take on the problem of the child's aggression. In the case of a child who has generally not exhibited aggressive behavior in the past, it is likely that the aggression is truly an expression of the child's anxiety and will pass when the anxiety is improved. In either case, it may be better to maintain the focus on the child's anxiety and the parents' accommodation.

In some situations, however, ignoring the child's aggression may not be a reasonable option. For example, when the child's behavior puts another person, such as a sibling, at risk, or when the child's behavior was so serious that it seems impossible to ignore, or when parents simply feel too strongly about the importance of addressing the aggression directly. In these situations, it becomes important for the therapist to suggest parental responses that also achieve the aims of not further escalating the aggression and of maintaining the focus on the child's anxiety and on reducing accommodation.

Nonescalating Response

Even when parents feel that their child's aggression must be addressed, it is still important to acknowledge that the behavior is a result of the child's anxiety and that the parents have chosen to change their behavior in a way that is challenging for the child. A useful means of directly addressing the behavior in this context is through the use of additional individuals from outside the immediate nuclear family. Parents can enlist the help of others from outside the home, and these individuals can convey to the child that they are aware of the aggressive behavior. These "supporters" can convey to the child that they understand the child's distress and empathize with it but that the aggressive behavior is not acceptable. For most children, receiving this message from multiple people from outside the home is a powerful experience and one that makes it considerably less likely that the aggression will repeat. The message to the child can be delivered in a supportive manner that makes it clear that the child is not being shamed or attacked but that boundaries of appropriate behavior must be maintained.

This form of addressing a child's aggression may seem counterintuitive to some parents (or indeed to some therapists) as it is not directly punitive of the child. However, it is more likely to be effective in reducing the aggressive behavior than most "punishments," and it achieves the important goal of addressing the aggression while also explicitly acknowledging the distress that caused it.

COPING WITH THREATS TO THE SELF

Children sometimes respond to changes in parental accommodation with threats against themselves. These can include explicit threatening statements such as "If you do this I will kill myself"; gestures such as holding a knife and implying they will harm themselves; or expressing verbally that they do not wish to live anymore under these circumstances. As with the case of aggressive behaviors, these can occur both in children who have a history of suicidal verbalizations and gestures and in children who have no prior history of similar behaviors. Such threats to the self can have a paralyzing effect on both parents and therapists. And even though the actual risk of self-harm as a result of parents modifying their accommodation behavior is low, therapists need to be prepared to navigate these difficult situations if they are to avoid allowing the child's threats to curtail an important part of the therapeutic process. A useful approach can incorporate elements of understanding the child's behavior and realistic assessment of risk, along with protecting the child while continuing to adhere to the goal of reducing accommodation.

Understanding the Child's Behavior

In most cases, the child's threats of self-harm are better understood as an expression of anxiety and frustration rather than as an expression of actual suicidal intent. Of course, the risks should never be taken lightly. But neither is it sensible to assume that every child who voices a threat to themselves is at imminent risk of physical harm. Considerations such as past history, seriousness and specificity of the threat, the manner and context in which it was expressed, and behaviors of the child when calm can all help inform this assessment. When the assessment suggests that the immediate risk to the child is low, the therapist can help parents to extricate themselves from paralysis by interpreting the child's words for them. For example, suggesting that their child is not actually saying that they intend to harm themselves but rather that they want the parent to know how difficult this is for them or how upset the parental actions have made them.

Protecting the Child's Safety While Continuing to Reduce Accommodation

These two goals, of protecting the child's safety and of reducing the parental accommodation, may seem contradictory. In reality, they are not. It is only the child's use of self-harm as a threat that makes it seem as though parents must choose between their child's safety and reducing accommodation. The child's threat seems to equate accommodation reduction with higher risk, but this is false. Parents acting supportively to help a child overcome an anxiety problem are very unlikely to be increasing the risk of the child's safety. Once the illusion that reducing accommodation increases risk is dispensed, it becomes easier to identify practical ways of achieving both aims concurrently. The aim of protecting the child from harm and the aim of helping the child by reducing accommodation can both be advanced simultaneously.

The therapist can suggest simple and practical ways of advancing both of these goals. For example, the therapist can suggest to parents that they maintain the child's safety by keeping the child under observation at home, in response to the threat of self-harm, while also continuing to refrain from accommodating. This watch-keeping can be organized and systematic. For example, parents can arrange for "shifts" during which one parent, or even additional people, take responsibility for observing the child. Alternatively, parents can respond to the threat of self-harm by visiting a hospital emergency room to have the child's safety professionally assessed and then continue with the accommodation reduction plan upon returning home. Essentially, the parents are disentangling each of the important aims from each other and acting independently to advance each one. Viewing the two aims as separate in this way makes it easier to see that the choice to protect their child does not have to equate to reverting to unhelpful accommodations that maintain anxiety. The therapist can explain to worried parents that actual suicidal behavior is more likely to be the result of a child feeling that there is no hope of overcoming the anxiety or that nobody is concerned or knowledgeable enough to help them overcome it than to result from parents acting in a determined manner to help their child, even if that help takes a form that the child does not like.

Case Examples

*Addressing Family Accommodation
Within Child Therapy*

10

Teenager with Generalized Anxiety Disorder

PRESENTATION

Heather was a 14-year-old, White English-speaking girl. Heather divided her time between her divorced parents, Christian and Stella. She had one younger brother, Luke. Heather presented with complaints relating to excessive worries and changes in her physical and emotional well-being. Heather's worries comprised a broad range of topics including her health and that of her brother, her grades and scholastic performance, losing things she might need, being late, her physical appearance, her social status and the worry that she would lose friends or that they do not really like her, and worrying about making the wrong decision when faced with even trivial choices. Heather was prone to outbursts, both of anger and of crying. Her anger was limited largely to the home environment, but the crying would happen at school as well. Heather had been eating poorly for several months and was complaining that she was not able to sleep at night. She frequently complained of headaches or backaches and recently had begun chewing on her collar or her hair.

For the past months, Heather had also shown signs of deteriorating mood. She seemed to be losing interest in the things she had always enjoyed, such as swimming and spending time with friends. She had decided not to continue with fencing, which had long been a passion of hers, and when Stella or Christian took her and Luke somewhere for fun, she seemed distant and remote. Only her grades still seemed important to her, though she rarely took pride in her excellent accomplishments, and in place of the activities she used to enjoy, she was spending much of her time sleeping or playing video games. Heather was also crying more often than usual and seemed slower to do things, moving with a kind of lethargy that had not been typical of her in the past.

Heather was accommodated by her parents in numerous ways. She sought constant reassurance when feeling worried, asking many questions throughout the day, particularly of Stella. Stella would often find herself answering the same question again and again or sitting with Heather and listening to her enumerating her many worried thoughts. Because Heather had difficulty making decisions, Christian and Stella would either avoid situations that would require a decision to be made (such as going out to eat or picking a movie to go to) or would make the decisions for her. When Heather did have to make a decision on her own, she would ask one of her parents for affirmation many times, even after the decision had been made. For example, when choosing a new article of clothing, Heather would deliberate for a long time, sometimes returning home without buying anything and then repeatedly ask her mother if she thought she had made the right choice.

Christian and Stella also accommodated Heather by screening her from any information they thought might trigger her anxiety and make her worried. When Stella's mother had surgery to replace her hip, Stella kept the information from Heather until her grandmother was home from the hospital and recuperating well. And when Christian began seeing another woman, he went to great lengths to shield Heather from this fact for as long as possible, fearing that it would upset her.

EVALUATION

Heather met diagnostic criteria for generalized anxiety disorder and for major depressive disorder. She was a highly intelligent young woman, who had scored mostly in the superior range in prior neuropsychological evaluation. As a baby she had developed normally, though was always described as "fussy." Her parents had divorced amicably when Heather was nine and her younger brother Luke was seven. Neither parent had ever suffered from any psychological disorder, but second-degree relatives on both sides had various anxiety and mood disorders, the most serious being a paternal grandfather with bipolar disorder.

Heather had been treated individually and as part of family therapy in the period of time surrounding her parents' divorce and, more recently, had been working with a therapist on her anxiety but felt that the treatment was not helpful. The therapist, whom Heather had seen for approximately three months, suggested to the parents that they try something else because she did not feel she was able to connect well with Heather.

During the evaluation, Heather was collaborative, responding openly to questions and acknowledging that her anxiety and depression had been getting worse. She initially avoided eye contact but was able to maintain eye contact when the clinician commented on it and asked if she felt uncomfortable.

Heather described her brain as being "a very restless place" and said that she "felt like there was never any turning it off," adding "I'll be at a friend's house, and everyone is talking or laughing, and I'm trying to look like them, but inside I'm just thinking about something else, and then I'll feel sad because I remember when I also could just hang out and have fun."

Heather scored in the clinical range on standardized measures of both anxiety and depression. On the Pediatric Anxiety Rating Scale (PARS), her score was

24, and on the child and parent versions of the Multimodal Anxiety Scale for Children (MASC), Heather and her parents (who completed the form together) rated her 110 and 102, respectively. Heather and her parents also indicated high levels of family accommodation on the Family Accommodation Scale–Anxiety (FASA). Their scores were 20 and 32, respectively.

Based on all of the information gathered, the therapist recommended cognitive-behavioral therapy for Heather, focused on her anxiety and depression, and the SPACE Program with her parents to target the family accommodation. Christian and Stella indicated they preferred to do the parent work together and felt confident that, despite their divorce, they could work well together.

TREATMENT COURSE

During the initial parts of Heather's work, treatment focused on psychoeducation and providing Heather with information about anxiety and depression and about the rationale for cognitive-behavioral therapy. Heather's previous recent therapy had included a strong emphasis on art and creativity, and Heather responded well to the idea of gaining more practical skill for coping with her challenges. Together with the therapist, Heather decided to focus first on her anxiety, because she felt that improving the anxiety would help her to feel happier as well and because she believed the anxiety was causing her the most interference in her daily life.

Heather was a compliant patient and followed the therapist's recommendation to keep a log of her worried thoughts during the week. The therapist also recommended that Heather begin practicing daily relaxation, and Heather found a mobile phone app that she liked to use for this.

The therapist next introduced the concepts of exposure and the importance of resisting avoidance in overcoming anxiety. Together, they came up with an exposure hierarchy that included doing things such as making time-limited decisions even if she felt unsure and arriving a few minutes late to class or other events.

After a few sessions with Heather, the therapist began also working with the parents, meeting with them immediately following the session with Heather. Heather was apprehensive about this because she feared that the therapist would divulge too much of her session to the parents and because she knew the parent work would include a focus on reducing the family accommodation. The therapist spoke with her about confidentiality and reassured her that her privacy would be respected as much as possible, as long this did not pose a safety risk. The therapist also suggested having one meeting with Heather and her parents together to set the stage for the parent work and to discuss the accommodations that would be targeted. During that session, the therapist began by praising the work that Heather was doing in therapy and then raising the topic of family accommodation.

THERAPIST: *I want you to know how much I enjoy meeting with Heather. She's such a model patient! I wish all my patients worked so hard. She's been really invested in this treatment, and I think it's already starting to pay off. What do you think Heather?*

HEATHER: *I guess.*

THERAPIST: *Tell me what you think has been most helpful so far?*

HEATHER: *Just keeping track of everything I think. And I'm a little less worried about being late since we did that.*

STELLA: *Thank you, doctor, we really do see a difference. And Heather never objects to coming here. In the past, we used to have to nag a bit to get her to go to therapy. She's been much better about it here.*

THERAPIST: *That's great! I appreciate you saying that. What did you mean when you said you see a difference?*

CHRISTIAN: *Well, she's still really anxious and down, but like Heather said, she doesn't freak out about being late every day. On days when I drive her, she used to wake up and start in right away about how we have to get going. Recently, it's been more relaxed.*

THERAPIST: *Great, and Stella, is that also what you meant, or did you have something else in mind?*

STELLA: *Well that, and also, I think she's been having fewer outbursts. Not as touchy.*

THERAPIST: *That's really good to hear. What do you think Heather? Do you feel like you're less touchy than you used to be?*

HEATHER: *I don't know . . . maybe . . . probably.*

THERAPIST: *OK! Well the other thing I wanted us to talk about today was about you guys. Heather is doing her work, and part of our plan is for you to be doing yours as well, right?*

STELLA: *Yes, I know . . . what should we be doing? We want to help her any way we can.*

THERAPIST: *I know you do, and I think you're going to be a huge help. When we met a few weeks ago we talked about some of the ways that Heather's anxiety affects you as well, like answering all those questions or leaving early to be on time.*

CHRISTIAN: *Her other therapist said children with generalized anxiety don't have trust and that we need to build that trust before she can feel OK. That's what I've been trying to do.*

THERAPIST: *Well, that's interesting. I've always had the impression that Heather trusts you a lot. More than a lot of kids I work with, actually. Heather, what do you think about that?*

HEATHER: *About what?*

THERAPIST: *Do you think you're anxious because it's hard for you to trust your parents?*

HEATHER: *No.*

THERAPIST: *Can you explain a bit more? No, you don't agree with that?*

HEATHER: *I trust them. I just get worried all the time. It's not their fault. I never said it was their fault. [teary]*

THERAPIST: *Thanks, Heather. That was said well. And you're right, you never said it was your parents' fault at all. Nobody's saying you did.*

THERAPIST: *[to parents] Sometimes that might be true, in some kids, but I think Heather trusts you a lot more than she trusts herself. In fact, if anything she trusts you too much, if there is such a thing. I want to help her trust more in herself and not need you quite as much.*

STELLA: *So how do we do that?*

THERAPIST: *So, as I was saying, we talked about all those things you do to help her. And I know that's what you've been doing, trying to help her. But, sometimes when we're trying to help, we actually do the opposite of what a child needs. Sometimes, by giving one thing we can make it harder to get something else—like if you give someone painkillers when what they really need is antibiotics. They're going to feel more comfortable, but they won't actually get healthy. Their body is telling them, I need medicine, and we're turning off that signal with the painkillers. Do you see what I mean?*

CHRISTIAN: *Like giving her a calculator so she won't learn to do arithmetic.*

THERAPIST: *Exactly! That's a really good metaphor. Better than antibiotics. If you give a kid a calculator from day one, it's easier but they probably won't learn to do math.*

HEATHER: *[mumbles something]*

THERAPIST: *What, Heather?*

HEATHER: *Always with the math. He loves math.*

THERAPIST: *[laughs] OK, forget the math. I think you get the point. When you help Heather in the ways we talked about, she's also missing out on something important. Heather, do you know what that thing is?*

HEATHER: *I don't know . . .*

THERAPIST: *You're missing out on learning that you can be OK without the help— that even if you're feeling really worried, you can still be ok. In fact, not only could you be ok without those things, but you might stop worrying sooner—like if you got the antibiotic you'd get healthier sooner. I think your brain is learning how to handle anxiety much better, through the great work that you've been doing here. And we need to let your brain practice those new skills. If your parents are always stepping in, it's not going to get much practice, right?*

HEATHER: *I guess . . . but what will they do?*

THERAPIST: *Let's talk about that. I have a couple of ideas, but I'd like to hear what all of you think as well.*

STELLA: *Maybe answering her questions?*

HEATHER: *Mom! I knew you were going to say that!*

THERAPIST: *Why did you think your mom would make that suggestion?*

HEATHER: *Because she thinks it's annoying.*

STELLA: *I don't think it's annoying, Heather. I'm trying to answer the doctor's question. We just want to help you OK?*

THERAPIST: *I think I'd probably find it annoying! Don't you, Heather?*

HEATHER: *I know it is. I'm sorry. [puts face down]*

THERAPIST: *Sure, it can be annoying. But that doesn't mean your mom is mad at you. Or that that's why she made that suggestion. I think she would do lots of annoying things to help you if you needed her too. Isn't that right, Stella?*

STELLA: *Of course.*

THERAPIST: *Exactly. Sometimes kids need things that are annoying. That's not their fault. It doesn't mean they're being bad. Nobody's mad at you Heather. By the way, this is not a Heather thing; it's an anxiety thing. Do you know what that means?*

HEATHER: *Not really.*

THERAPIST: *It means that we understand that when you're asking a million questions, it's not because Heather wants to be annoying. It's because your anxiety is making you feel like you have to, right?*

HEATHER: *Yes.*

THERAPIST: *And it also means that every kid with anxiety does the same thing. I don't know if I told you that. But it's true. I help lots of kids who are anxious, and you know what they all have in common? When they get anxious, they want their parents to help. So they ask lots of worry questions and do all kinds of other things to feel better. This is not just you, Heather, or you, Stella and Christian. This is just the way anxiety works. So there's no point getting mad. Or, if you want to get mad, get mad at anxiety! That way we can all get mad at it together, and we'll beat it together, OK?*

OTHERS: *OK.*

THERAPIST: *So Stella suggested working on the questions. Any other ideas before we choose?*

CHRISTIAN: *Maybe her sleep?*

THERAPIST: *Tell me what you mean about her sleep.*

CHRISTIAN: *Well, she stays up really late, just thinking about stuff. Sometimes I find her awake really, really late, and I know it just makes her feel worse. I'd like her to get more rest.*

THERAPIST: *Yes, sleep is important. So what do you do when she's not sleeping?*

CHRISTIAN: *Nothing. What can I do? I can't make her fall asleep, right?*

THERAPIST: *No, you definitely can't. Nobody can do that. So I think that's a good goal for Heather and me to work on together. I can try to teach her some things she can do to fall asleep better. But in terms of the things that you do, as parents, it sounds like the questions is an area where you'll be able to make more of a difference right?*

CHRISTIAN: *I guess . . .*

STELLA: *You sound like her now . . . "I guess". . .*

THERAPIST: *[chuckling] Maybe she's more like you than you think. So, Heather, how do you feel about your parents trying to work on this. Trying to answer fewer of your worry questions? Good idea or bad idea?*

HEATHER: *I don't know if I can do it.*

THERAPIST: *"If you can do what"—what do you mean?*

HEATHER: *If I can stop asking them those questions all the time. I just get really worried inside my head.*

THERAPIST: *Yes, I know you do. It's really uncomfortable too, isn't it? But you don't have to ask fewer questions. This is their homework, not yours. I'll make a plan with them for how they will answer less, and we'll let you know the plan ahead of time. But it won't be "Heather doesn't ask questions." Doesn't make sense for them to make that kind of a plan, does it? It will be more like "Mom and Dad only answer each question one time." We have to think about the details, and you'll have a chance to say what you think, but it will only be for what they do, OK?*

HEATHER: *I guess.*

STELLA: *See what I mean!*

THERAPIST: *So, we're all clear about this right? It's really important. This is only going to be homework for the two of you. Don't expect Heather to make it easy on you by not asking you questions. In fact, Heather, you have my permission to make it as hard as you want! You can really put them through the ringer, and let's see if they can take it. [smiling]*

CHRISTIAN: *Gee, thanks, doc.*

THERAPIST: *OK, sounds like we know where we're headed. You're all such a really great family! You're lucky to have one another, aren't you? And no saying "I guess!"*

Meeting alone with Christian and Stella, the therapist formulated a detailed plan for reducing the accommodation of answering Heather's worry questions. The plan focused on the afternoon hours because Heather had been feeling sadder in the mornings and because the parents were concerned about her getting "stuck" in the morning if they didn't answer. They were worried that between feeling like she needed them to answer and worrying about being late to school, Heather would just be too overwhelmed by anxiety and things would get out of hand. They also chose to focus at first only on worries relating to health and grades. These were the most common questions that Heather asked, and the therapist suggested that if they also tried to implement a plan about every other thought and worry that came up, it would be too hard for them to stay focused and remember not to accommodate. They agreed to have the same plan for both parents and to try to execute it in the same way in each of their houses. The plan they devised was as follows:

- Mom or Dad will only answer one question about health each day.
- This includes questions about Heather's health, her brother's health, or anyone else in the family.
- This also includes repetitions (or variations) of the same question. If they already answered once, they will not answer the same question again (or another question).
- Mom or Dad will also answer one question each day about grades and schoolwork.
- If Heather has a specific request or question about a current homework assignment and needs help, Mom or Dad will help her as appropriate but not answer additional questions that they think are anxiety questions.

- If Heather asks an anxiety question after Mom or Dad have already answered they will say, "Heather, I'm not answering more worry questions today. I know it's hard but I'm sure you'll be fine. Try to use what you learned in therapy."
- If Heather still persists with asking, Mom or Dad will say one time, "Heather, I know you're uncomfortable, but I'm not going to respond anymore. I love you." And then not respond at all to subsequent questions.
- If Heather is at Mom's house, she can still ask Dad one question as well, on the phone. Likewise, if Heather is at Dad's house.
- Questions over text or on the phone count. If Heather is asking over text message, Mom or Dad will reply with the same words as in person and then will not reply to the texts anymore.
- At the end of each day, Mom or Dad will praise Heather for coping with the plan and tell her how proud they are of her.

Christian and Stella showed the plan to Heather. They were surprised by her reaction. Heather giggled a little bit, and when they asked her why she was laughing she said, "Wow, it's like you worked this out with a lawyer." As the therapist had suggested, they asked Heather if she had any comments or suggestions she wanted to make before they started. Heather asked if it could be two questions instead of one each day. The parents and therapist had discussed this possibility in advance and they told her "OK, if you think two is better for you at first, we can do that instead."

At the next session the therapist reviewed with the parents how the plan had gone that week:

THERAPIST: *So, big week right? I'm curious to hear how things went for you.*
STELLA: *We had ups and downs.*
THERAPIST: *Tell me what you mean. And then I'd like to hear how it was for you as well, Christian, OK?*
STELLA: *Well, at first, I was really happy about her reaction. She actually laughed! She thought it was funny that we had this whole big plan written out. I don't think she expected that.*
THERAPIST: *I guess it really can be kind of funny though, right? I can see why she would think that.*
STELLA: *Yes, well . . . like you said, she wanted it to be more questions and not just one. Since she suggested two questions a day, we said OK, and she was very calm about it. So that was a relief.*
THERAPIST: *That's great, I'm glad none of the other things we talked about happened.*
STELLA: *The first day, Tuesday, went pretty much ok. I think she had a pretty good day at school because she was in a good mood when she came home. She didn't actually ask anything until around dinner time, and then when she saw that I was making hamburgers, she started worrying about fat and*

health and all that, and she asked me whether I had ever had my choles-terol checked. The first time caught me off guard, so I just said not recently. Then she asked me whether I didn't think it was bad not to check, and would I check. Then I remembered about the plan and after I answered her, I told her like we planned, "That's your last question for today, OK?" I could see it made her a little mad; she got this look. And she told me, "Oh, right, your stupid plan." But she stopped asking about it.

THERAPIST: *That's really great! Well done. It sounds like you did just like we planned: You answered the first two questions and then reminded her that you would not answer more.*

STELLA: *Later she started in with asking me about the GPA she would need to get into college. I told her, "Remember, just two questions. I already answered you today, so no more questions." I know I should have said, "No more answers, right?"*

THERAPIST: *Yes, it's great you realize that. How did she react?*

STELLA: *She said, "This is different." I asked her why it was different, and she said, "This is not just a worry," that she really needs to get into college. I told her that's true, but that worrying about it now is not really useful, and it sounds like a worry question to me. She got annoyed with me and said, 'You don't understand. You can't tell me why I think something." I told her that her anxiety was making her worried and that this was the plan we had all decided on, so she should just go get ready for bed. Heather wanted to call her dad and I said, "Sure, OK."*

CHRISTIAN: *She did call me and started talking about how her mom was being unfair to her. That's something she does sometimes.*

THERAPIST: *What do you usually say to that?*

CHRISTIAN: *I just tell her she needs to work stuff out with her mom and that I can't tell them how to do it.*

THERAPIST: *OK, what happened next?*

CHRISTIAN: *She asked me about the college, and I told her that a better GPA would help her, but that it's really going to be her grades later on that matter more and that she should just do her best and things would be fine.*

THERAPIST: *OK, was she OK with that?*

CHRISTIAN: *At first she was, but she did want to continue to talk about it, and in the end I told her, "Heather, enough questions now. It's time for you to get some sleep." She said I was just saying what her mom told me to say, but we hung up after that.*

THERAPIST: *OK, so how do you both think that went? Would you do anything differently?*

STELLA: *I know I could have been firmer.*

THERAPIST: *It sounds to me like you carried out the plan pretty well. The only thing that could make it easier is probably to not try to make her stop asking, to talk about "your plan" instead of "the plan you made together." It's true that she agreed to the plan, but most kids will still be unable to stick to it at first. No point getting annoyed with them for that, really. She just needs to see that you are willing to be firm about it. It's almost like she has no choice but to test it out a little. Once she sees that you are going to stick with it, it will be easier for her to stop asking.*

STELLA: *But we changed it to two questions because of her, didn't we?*

THERAPIST: *Yes, but that's still not going to mean she won't try to ask more. Remember, this is not Heather trying to ask just for fun. She's really anxious and feeling worried, and she knows from experience that you can help her feel better by answering her questions. It's natural for her to try to ask despite the plan.*

STELLA: *OK, the next day was similar, but Thursday things got a little heated. Let's just say it was not the best day.*

THERAPIST: *How so?*

STELLA: *Well, a couple of things happened. Her brother, Luke, was sick and that always makes her anxious. It's nothing serious, just a flu or a cold, but she gets worried. And she had a math test at school that she thinks didn't go well, even though she doesn't even have the grade back yet. So she started in as soon as she came home from school. How do we know that it's just a cold? Did we take him to the doctor? What if it's something more serious? And also with the test. What about if she failed? All her teachers will think she's stupid. And she won't get into college. And she thinks she wants to be vet, so what about if she doesn't get into a program because of her grades. On and on. I answered her two questions, maybe one or two more even, but she wouldn't stop. I suggested she call her dad again, but that just made her even angrier. She said she knows we're working together against her. I told her to use what she learned from you, but she said she hasn't learned anything, and it's all just stupid and a waste of time. She said she wouldn't come to today's session because you're just trying to make things worse for her.* [Heather did come to the session, which was to occur directly following the parent session.] *I started to get angry with her as well. I really needed to take care of Luke, and she was being so aggravating and yelling at me. I told her if she was not going to let us follow the plan and didn't use the therapy at all, then it's wasting our time and money to come here. I shouldn't have said that, I know, but she made me really mad. It seemed selfish for her to be acting like this when her brother is sick. She says she's so worried about him, but she won't let him sleep. Like he needs to hear her yelling that maybe he's seriously sick when he's feeling so bad!*

THERAPIST: *That sounds like a pretty rough afternoon. How did it all end?*

STELLA: *In the end, I just said, "Heather, enough is enough. I have other things I need to take care of and you're being impossible. Just leave me alone until you're calm." She was angry, but she went in her room and stayed there for a while and when she came out she was sulky, but she helped me with dinner and things were calmer.*

THERAPIST: *So you were able to stick to not answering her anymore?*

STELLA: *Yes, but she was really mad at me. I didn't know if she would come today or not. We had a couple of other fights like that over the week, and*

I know she's feeling really mad about the whole thing. Maybe we should all talk about it together again? She really listened when you explained it to her.

CHRISTIAN: *It was similar over the weekend at my house. Most of the time she was OK, but she got upset with me when I suggested we all watch a movie together because she said she needs to study and then she started in with questions and got mad at me for not answering. She said she wants to go back to her mom's house, which she never did before. I told her it was OK if Stella agrees but that I really look forward to our time together. She stayed, but it was definitely tough.*

THERAPIST: *Well, I'm really impressed that you both were able to stick to the plan despite it being so hard. I have the feeling I should have prepared you better for how challenging it can be. Maybe it was unfair to put you in that position without you realizing what to expect. Her reactions are actually pretty typical for an anxious child. It's almost inevitable that there will be rough days like that. It's rare that that doesn't happen. But there is one thing you can do to make those times shorter and to help them end sooner.*

STELLA: *What's that?*

THERAPIST: *The less you engage with her when she's trying to get you to answer, the sooner it will stop. I know you feel bad for her in those moments but trying to get her to stop asking is probably just making it harder for all of you. Think about it like this: When she wants you to answer a question, everything you say apart from answering the question itself just sounds to her like an argument. It makes her feel like if she can just come up with a good enough argument, she might convince you to answer. So, she has no choice but to keep trying. And as she keeps on trying she is going to get more and more frustrated that it's not working. When you disengage completely, she will realize that there really is nothing to say about it at all. And then she'll feel frustrated for a while, but it will make it easier for her to stop. So by responding to her, you're actually making it harder to stop, and the anxiety will just feel worse and worse. Do you understand what I mean?*

CHRISTIAN: *Like when she wants us to buy a new video game, and she'll keep pestering and pestering until we say yes.*

THERAPIST: *Right! If you keep answering her, even if what you are saying is "No," she still feels like as long as the conversation keeps going there's a chance to turn the "no" into "yes." Kids get this very instinctively—that if we're still talking about it there's hope. Imagine if instead of asking you for a video game, she was asking you to buy her a pony, or to move to a giant mansion, or something unrealistic like that. You would probably just say, "Of course not!" and if she kept asking, you would probably realize that debating it is pointless because those are totally unrealistic things. And that would make it easier for her to give up the idea as well. She might still want that pony, but she wouldn't keep asking for it if she saw you were completely serious and weren't even talking about it anymore. It's the same thing with her anxiety. If you're answering her, it makes her feel like there's still a chance, and she'll have to keep asking. And everyone ends up feeling worse in the end.*

STELLA: *But how do we not answer her? We can't just ignore her, right?*

THERAPIST: *I think in the end you did that though, didn't you? You told her, "Leave me alone," and she saw you were serious and she did.*

STELLA: *Because I was mad. I don't want to have to get mad at her and push her away like that.*

THERAPIST: *Right, of course you don't want that. And that's not what I'm suggesting. But you can tell her the same thing in a calm way, too. The thing is there is really nothing you can say that will make her stop. It's you that has to stop the argument. I'm not saying you should ignore her. Just ignore those questions. If she wants to talk about something else, of course, you'll be there and happy to talk to her. Let's try to think of some things you can say when you're going to stop answering her, so she knows you're not mad. How about "Heather, I think if I keep answering you we're both going to get upset so I'm just going to ignore these questions now, but I get that you're anxious and I'm not mad." Remember the supportive statements? You could say "I know you're anxious, but I'm sure you'll be OK, and this argument is only making us both feel worse so I'm going to stop my side of it. We can talk about anything else that you want, but I get it if you don't feel like you can stop asking me just yet. I'm sure you'll feel ready soon." That way you're explicitly giving her permission to keep asking you, and you're making it your job to not answer. You're showing her that you understand it's too hard for her to stop right away, and I think it will help you get less mad at her if you remind yourself of that.*

STELLA: *OK, I can try that.*

THERAPIST: *Great! Can we role-play that a little?*

STELLA: *Umm . . . sure . . . how do you mean?*

THERAPIST: *I'll be Heather, and I'll ask you some questions. Let's make-believe you already answered me twice and now you're going to try to disengage. OK? Ready?*

STELLA: *OK, so just me or both of us?*

THERAPIST: *Let's do it with both of you, one at a time because that's how it will usually be in real life. Can you go first?*

STELLA: *OK.*

THERAPIST: *So, I'm Heather now. Mom, enough with your stupid plan already. I told you it doesn't help me OK? Just tell me if I'm ready or I need to study more, OK? It's not a big deal, and you're just making everything worse!*

STELLA: *Wow, it's like you've been in our house!*

THERAPIST: *Well, Heather is a very special girl. But her anxiety is actually pretty typical. This is just what anxiety does. So back to the role play. Mom! Can you just tell me this one thing, and I promise I won't ask anymore today.*

STELLA: *Heather, baby, I love you, and I know you're feeling really worried about your test, but it doesn't help for me to answer these things so just figure it out on your own, and you'll be fine.*

THERAPIST: *But I need your help! Don't you want to help me?*

STELLA: *Of course, I do want to help you. But this is how I'm trying to help you, OK?*

THERAPIST: *But it's not helping me at all! You can help me by just telling me if I'm ready. Just tell me I'm ready, and I'll be able to stop.*

STELLA: *I know you think that, but we've tried that loads of times. It's never just the one thing, is it?*

THERAPIST: *OK, Stella, do you see what's going on here?*

STELLA: *I keep answering her.*

THERAPIST: *Exactly! We're programmed to answer when spoken to. It's our reflex and especially when it's our child. But I want you to try to not answer at all. Here's something you can use: When you hear her asking you a question or trying to draw you in to the debate, try to repeat a phrase in your head over and over again, like a mantra. How about something like "I don't need to say anything" or "She'll be fine" or maybe just "Stay calm and don't answer!" like the "keep calm" stickers you see all over. OK, ready to try again?*

STELLA: *[sighs] OK . . .*

THERAPIST: *Mom, can you just tell me this one thing. You always told me you would help me with schoolwork if I try and do my part. So that's what I'm trying to do and I need your help.*

STELLA: *[mumbles]*

THERAPIST: *Hello!! Mom! Are you there??? What are you mumbling?*

STELLA: *Just something to help me stay cool.*

THERAPIST: *You look like a weirdo! Did Dr. S. tell you to do this? Another great idea you came up with? Seriously, I think I should go back to my old therapist. At least she tried to help!*

STELLA: *[laughs and then continues to mumble]*

THERAPIST: *Good for you! OK, I tried my best, and you were able to not answer. I'm sure if you do that at home these arguments will fade away pretty soon. You'll see. When Heather knows there's no getting an answer out of you, she'll move on much faster. She might not thank you right away, but let me handle her being angry for now, OK? I can take it. And she will thank you when she's a lot less worried! Christian, you ready for your turn? Let's see if you can stick with it as well.*

CHRISTIAN: *Let's go!*

Heather was reluctant in her own session to disclose the difficulty that her parents' reduced accommodation was causing but opened up when she realized her parents had already spoken about it with the therapist. She voiced her frustration but acknowledged that she still thought her parents were probably making the right choice. She felt guilty for making them angry at her and became teary when she talked about her mom yelling at her to "leave me alone." The therapist emphasized again that Heather's job was not to refrain from asking the questions and that it was her parents' responsibility to cope with it. The therapist reminded Heather she had "permission" to make it hard for them and so she had nothing to feel guilty about. Her parents may have forgotten, but they had agreed to the plan, and it was their job to carry it out despite her questions.

Over the rest of her therapy, Heather continued to work on cognitive restructuring and exposures, and Stella and Christian took on additional accommodation reduction goals. After that first week, both parents improved in their ability to disengage from Heather when she became "stuck" in her questions, and Stella made use of the mantra—repeating to herself "Stay calm and don't answer" again and again. As a result, Heather soon began to ask fewer questions and, by the third week of the plan, would sometimes not even ask the two questions that each parent was "allowed" to answer. The parents debated reducing the goal to one answer but felt it was not really necessary in light of the change in Heather and opted to move on to another goal instead.

By the end of therapy, Heather no longer met criteria for generalized anxiety disorder, and her depression was significantly improved as well. Her scores on the MASC were greatly reduced, with her self-rating and her parents' rating being 42 and 35, respectively. Her FASA accommodation scores were also significantly reduced (8 and 12, for child and parent ratings, respectively). Heather no longer met criteria for major depression but continued to show signs of anhedonia and although she had many fewer emotional outbursts, she still became tearful several times per week. The family debated with the therapist starting a course of antidepressants but decided to wait and continue with the cognitive-behavioral therapy, now focused on depression, as this was Heather's preference.

11

Child with Separation Anxiety Disorder

PRESENTATION

Yuki was a seven-year-old Japanese-American boy and an only child. Yuki's parents, Kenta and Hiroko, were both born in Japan, where they met and married and had been living in the United States for 11 years. Yuki was fluent in English and Japanese, both of which were spoken in the home.

Yuki's parents described fears relating to separation, which had worsened since Yuki started the second grade, approximately two months prior to the initial evaluation. Yuki had difficulty being away from his mother and, to a lesser extent, his father. He would follow his mother from room to room, would not sleep in his own bedroom unless his mother slept with him, and avoided all play dates unless his mother stayed with him for the duration of the visit. Yuki had tried to go to a chess class, a game he excelled at, but when, at the second session, his mother attempted to leave, Yuki became very upset and cried loudly, and his mother had to take him home. After that, Yuki refused to continue with the class, and he participated in no other out of school activities. Yuki also refused to shower unless one of his parents stayed in the room with him, and he delayed going to the bathroom as long as possible, which had led to several accidents. Hiroko worked from home and was able to spend most of the day with Yuki, but she felt that her productivity was diminished because of his constantly being in the same room and talking to her. She had also given up going for runs during the day, her preferred form of exercise, because Yuki made a scene if she tried to leave, even if her assistant, who was happy to double as a babysitter, was in the house. The family presented for evaluation due to a further exacerbation in Yuki's anxiety, which had started the previous week. Kenta had dropped Yuki off at school as usual, but after one hour the school had called Hiroko to say that Yuki was not feeling well. When she went to pick him up, Yuki told Hiroko that he had been feeling worried about her not picking him up and it had "made him sick." He agreed to stay in school if Yuki stayed on the school grounds. This had recurred another time since the first event, and the school had recommended that the family seek treatment for childhood anxiety.

EVALUATION

Yuki met diagnostic criteria for separation anxiety disorder. There was no previous testing, but Yuki was clearly an intelligent child, who achieved good grades in all his classes. A referral letter from the school psychologist raised the possibility that Yuki may have autism spectrum disorder. However, no evidence was provided to support this hypothesis, and the therapist did not identify any symptoms of autism. The therapist did administer an autism spectrum disorder screening questionnaire to the parents, and their responses placed Yuki in the "low probability" range.

Yuki had developed normally as a baby, achieving developmental milestones in the normal time range. The only remarkable thing in the parents' description of Yuki's early development was the very early onset of separation anxiety symptoms. Hiroko and Kenta had first attempted to place Yuki in a nursery school, for the morning only, when he was 10 months old. Yuki had cried persistently for the first few days, and the parents decided to postpone the issue and to try again the following year. This pattern repeated several times, with repeated attempts to enroll Yuki in school, followed by intense and persistent crying and the parents relenting and postponing the decision.

When Yuki was four years old, Kenta and Hiroko decided to enroll him in a prekindergarten classroom "at all costs." Hiroko stayed in the class with him for the first few days and then waited in the hallway for the following days. Yuki again had difficulty separating, clinging to his mother when she tried to leave the classroom or to have him enter without her. With much difficulty, Yuki did ultimately become accustomed to the class and after a few weeks appeared to be enjoying the time there, though he continued to cling and cry during the separation on many mornings. During the first year of school, things were a little easier, and the parents were hopeful that they had "turned the corner" with regards to his separation anxiety, though out of school he remained extremely anxious and avoidant of any separation. He had continued to attend school with relatively little disruption until the week prior to evaluation.

Yuki was cheerful and energetic during the evaluation but refused to separate from his mother for even a few minutes. He consented to his father leaving the room while he remained with his mother but not the other way around. Yuki responded to the assessment questions and was able to complete standardized measures of anxiety and accommodation with the therapist helping him to read the questions and explaining words he did not know. Yuki endorsed all the symptoms of separation anxiety disorder, including feeling "bad" and "scared" when not with his mother, worrying about separation and imagining that "bad things" would happen if he were not with her, avoiding going places without his mother, and having nightmares if he did not sleep next to one of his parents.

When asked about the "bad things" that could happen if he were not with his mother Yuki struggled to answer but said, "She might not come back . . . ever" and "Something could happen to me. . . . I don't know . . . like a bad man." He was not able to describe the content of his nightmares but said they were about "being alone" or "going away."

Yuki's scores on a measure of anxiety, the Screen for Child Anxiety Related Emotional Disorders (SCARED; Birmaher et al., 1997), were elevated based on both his and mother's ratings with the highest score for the separation anxiety subscale (14 and 13, respectively). Family accommodation was also rated high by his mother (total score of 30), though Yuki himself rated only moderate accommodation (score of 16).

Based on the information gathered, the therapist initially recommended only cognitive-behavioral therapy for Yuki, who agreed to participate on the condition that his mother would be with him in the room. The therapist agreed to begin treatment in this way but made it clear that this should be temporary and that Yuki would hopefully soon be feeling capable of having at least part of a session without a parent present. The therapist also asked Hiroko to remain quiet during the session unless specifically asked to participate, and Hiroko agreed to do so.

TREATMENT COURSE

The therapist began the treatment by building rapport and providing Yuki with psychoeducation about anxiety and cognitive-behavioral therapy. In the second half of the session the therapist introduced a "daily diary" that Yuki would be filling out with the help of his parents, as needed. The diary would include details about anxiety problems he had encountered that day, including the situation, his physical reactions, and the thoughts he had when feeling scared.

In their next two sessions, the therapist reviewed the daily diaries and introduced the different ways that anxiety affects a child, including their body, their thoughts, and their actions. Using an example from the daily diary, Yuki and the therapist talked about how each of these were affected when he felt scared. The therapist then introduced the concept of avoidance and the importance of practicing exposures, both in session and between therapy sessions. Yuki was engaged and collaborative during these sessions and worked with the therapist on creating an anxiety hierarchy with exposures he would practice over the course of therapy.

Yuki's first in-session exposure was for his mother to leave the therapy office for five minutes, which occurred in the latter part of his third session. The therapist asked Hiroko to return after the agreed upon time regardless of Yuki's behavior in response to the separation. Yuki handled this initial exposure well and reported feeling only moderate anxiety. When his mother returned, she praised him for coping so well. For his first out-of-session exposure, Yuki and the therapist planned that he would go upstairs to his room for five minutes while his mother waited downstairs. Yuki was to practice this each day, during the daytime hours. At the end of the session, the therapist engaged Hiroko in the conversation as well to ensure she understood the plan and to encourage her to remind Yuki to practice each day.

At the following session, Yuki initially stated that he had completed the exposures as planned, but his mother gave the therapist a look and shook her head to indicate she disagreed.

THERAPIST: *That's great to hear, Yuki. Can you tell me how that went for you?*

YUKI: *I went up to my room for five minutes.*

HIROKO: *[Says something in Japanese]*

THERAPIST: *Yuki, what is your mother saying? Can you tell me? It's so great that you know two languages, but I'm afraid I only know about three words in Japanese.*

YUKI: *She said I didn't do it right.*

HIROKO: *That's not how I said it, I just said . . .*

THERAPIST: *[interrupting] Just a second Hiroko, I'd actually like to hear what Yuki thinks you meant, if that's OK? Yuki, what do you think your mother was trying to say?*

YUKI: *It's because I called her to come up.*

THERAPIST: *OK, why don't you just tell me how it went? Let's make believe I was watching a movie of you practicing your exposure. What would I see?*

YUKI: *Not a very good movie. Nobody would go to that.*

THERAPIST: *[laughs] Maybe I would! But right now, it's the most interesting movie there is. Better than* Star Wars! *So just tell me what the movie shows.*

YUKI: *OK, scene one . . . [laughs, therapist and Hiroko laugh as well], Mama told me it was time to practice. I said OK, and I went up.*

HIROKO: *[stifles a cough] It took a little more than that!*

THERAPIST: *OK, let's get his description first. I'm sure you'll have plenty to add. OK Yuki, go on . . .*

YUKI: *Scene two . . . I went to my room, but the light was off.*

THERAPIST: *Was it dark in the room? Had the sun gone down already?*

YUKI: *No, but I don't like to be there with the light off. So I called mama to turn on the light.*

THERAPIST: *OK, did she come?*

YUKI: *At first she didn't, but then she did.*

THERAPIST: *OK, what's scene three.*

YUKI: *So we stayed there for five minutes.*

THERAPIST: *You stayed there with mama?*

YUKI: *Yes.*

THERAPIST: *Got it. And did mama think that was the best plan, or did she have a different idea?*

YUKI: *She wanted to go back down.*

THERAPIST: *And you didn't want her to?*

YUKI: *No, I made her stay.*

THERAPIST: *Wow, you "made her"? How do you make her do stuff? Is there a trick to that?*

YUKI: *I just did. She can tell you.*

THERAPIST: *OK, I'll ask her. But first tell me about the other days. Did you practice more times?*

YUKI: *Yes, I did it two more times. No, three more times.*

HIROKO: *Two more times.*

THERAPIST: *And how did those go, Yuki? Were they different or the same?*

YUKI: *Mama turned on the light before I went up.*

THERAPIST: *Great, good thinking. Did that make it any easier for you?*

YUKI: *Not really, I called her anyway. I was scared to be there by myself.*

THERAPIST: *Yes, I know it can feel really scary for you. These are tough things to practice, you're brave for trying. So, was Mama with you every time?*

YUKI: *[looks sheepish] Uh huh.*

THERAPIST: *OK, thanks for showing me that movie! You're a good director. Maybe you'll make real movies someday. Would you like that?*

YUKI: *[smiling now] Yes!*

THERAPIST: *OK, just make sure you save me a ticket, OK? So, can we hear a bit more from Mama's side now? Is that OK?*

HIROKO: *He doesn't want to do the practices, I have to tell him many times.*

THERAPIST: *OK, that's pretty typical. I'm glad you didn't give up.*

HIROKO: *And he didn't really stay in his room by himself at all. He finds a reason I need to be there, and he won't let me leave. If I try to leave, he holds on to me. I can't get him to agree to be by himself. I told him it can't work if he doesn't do it, right?*

THERAPIST: *It is really important. But I think we're forgetting something that's also very important. Can either of you guess what?*

YUKI: *No.*

THERAPIST: *That this was the first time! Nobody can be perfect on the first try! That makes no sense. Of course, it's hard at first. I think for a first attempt you both did really well, don't you?*

HIROKO: *I don't know.*

THERAPIST: *Of course you did! You did great at reminding Yuki and encouraging him, and even trying to leave him alone in the room. And Yuki, what do you think you did well?*

YUKI: *I don't know . . . going up?*

THERAPIST: *Exactly! You went upstairs. That means you tried! In fact, you tried at least three times! I think that's great! We should all be really happy about this. Mama, when was the last time Yuki even tried to go to a room by himself before this week?*

HIROKO: *Never, I think.*

THERAPIST: *So that's huge! He never did that at all, and now he tried three times in one week!*

HIROKO: *Right, but . . .*

THERAPIST: *No buts! You're feeling frustrated that he didn't actually stay by himself. I get it. But I could have told you last week that he probably wouldn't on his first try. Maybe it was a mistake not to say that, but I didn't want to lower the chances even more. Yuki's doing great. So I think we just need to keep trying, OK? This is a great first time. Let's see if we can have a great second time as well. Yuki, what do you think a good second time looks like?*

YUKI: *I actually stay five minutes?*

THERAPIST: *Well, that would be an awesome second time! I think even if you end up staying just some of it, we'll be happy. But definitely try for five minutes. And another thing that would make time two be really good is if you do it every day! Do you think that's possible?*

YUKI: *Yes.*

THERAPIST: *Terrific! Good plan. Now Mama, I do want you to keep encouraging Yuki to do it. You're allowed to nag him if needed, ok? But, remember, this is his exposure. So you can't actually force him to do it. Don't try to force him. If he needs some prodding, it's great for you to help. But no forcing him, OK? It's his homework.*

HIROKO: *OK, prodding, no forcing.*

THERAPIST: *Exactly! Prodding, no forcing. I think you'll be able to tell the difference. So we'll see how it goes, OK?*

At the following session Yuki and his mother again reported that Yuki had attempted the exposures (four times), but he had again refused to remain alone in the room for any duration of time. His mother had tried to offer him rewards for staying, such as treats or a toy, and Yuki initially agreed he would do it. But in the end, he had still refused to allow Hiroko to leave the room and had followed her out and clung to her when she tried to leave. The therapist decided to attempt to address the behavior through a change in family accommodation, as well as continuing the cognitive-behavioral work with Yuki. The therapist introduced this plan in a meeting with both Yuki and Hiroko.

THERAPIST: *OK, I've been thinking about these exposures, and I think I know why we've been having some difficulty with you actually staying alone in the room. I have an idea that might help. Can I tell you about it?*

HIROKO: *Of course.*

THERAPIST: *Well, it occurred to me that what we're trying to do might be just a bit too difficult for Yuki to take on.*

HIROKO: *You think we need a shorter time?*

THERAPIST: *That might help. We could ask Yuki what he thinks. But actually I had a different thought. One thing that might be making it difficult for Yuki to practice staying alone is that he has you right there! He has to actually choose to say "no" to something that's right there and can help him not feel scared. Yuki, I think that's a pretty hard thing to do. It's like if you were used to eating just sweets and chocolate at every meal. And you decided, this is not good, I really need to eat some healthier food, or I'll turn into a Mars Bar. So you decided at each meal you're going to eat something healthy. But then you sat down to eat and there were all the sweets, and candy, and ice* cream, and chocolate . . . and one little bowl of carrot sticks. What do you think you'd eat?

YUKI: The ice cream!

HIROKO: He definitely would!

THERAPIST: So would I! Who wouldn't? It's just so hard to pick the healthy food when all those sweets are right there! I think this might be similar. I know you want to pick to do the practice and be in the room without mom, but it's so hard when she's right there, isn't it?

YUKI: Because it's scary for me.

THERAPIST: Exactly! Because it's scary for you. And I know you remember that scary is different from dangerous right? And that when something is dangerous it helps us if we don't do it but that if something is scary but not dangerous, it helps us if we do it. But it's still scary because you haven't practiced yet. So choosing to practice when it's still scary and your mama is right there and can make it not scary is a really tough choice to make. Like with the food, it could be that if you ate those carrot sticks you'd say, "Mmm, these are actually pretty good," but you won't know if you don't taste them because of all those sweets. And when you start to practice the exposure you'll realize '"OK, this is not so bad," but you won't realize it if you can't practice because your mama is right there. Do you see what I mean?

YUKI: Yes, but I don't want her to leave!

THERAPIST: Of course not! Your mama loves you and is not going anywhere! I don't want her to leave you either! Of course she won't. But so far, I only told you the problem. I haven't told you the solution yet. Are you ready for the solution?

YUKI: OK.

THERAPIST: It's just like the food again. If your mama wanted to help you eat healthy food instead of all those sweets what would she do?

YUKI: Not give the sweets?

THERAPIST: Exactly! You're so smart! You could be doing my job instead of me! Because you get it already. If she wanted to help you, the best thing would be to make it her homework instead of yours. Like instead of your homework being "I'll eat the carrot sticks," her homework could be "I'll only give Yuki healthy food" or "I'll give healthy food first and just a sweet for dessert." Something like that. See, then you wouldn't have to make such a tough choice. She would have to do something instead. And if you got annoyed at her and said "but I want my ice cream," she would just say "I know you do, Yuki, but I think it's really important that you eat some healthy food." Gosh, I'm getting hungry from all this talk of food.

YUKI: Me too!

THERAPIST: Maybe after you leave here you and Mama can get something to eat. So I think the solution for the anxiety is sort of the same thing. Instead of us making it only your homework to practice being in the room alone, we could give mama some homework as well. What could her homework be, do you think?

YUKI: *To not come with me to the room?*

THERAPIST: *That's good thinking! But I want to keep the two homeworks separate. That way each of you can work on yours, and we can see who does the best homework. So your homework can be the exposure same as before, and you just keep trying. Eventually, you'll get it. I'm 100% sure about that! And your mama's homework could be sometimes leaving you in a room or going somewhere without you. We could start really small at first, so she doesn't have too hard a time, just like we are starting small with your homework.*

YUKI: *No.*

THERAPIST: *You're not loving this idea?*

YUKI: *No, because I don't want her to go.*

THERAPIST: *Of course, you don't. And I guarantee we can start really small. Here's my suggestion: Every day mama goes into her room for five minutes and closes the door. Do you think you can handle that? Five minutes with the door closed and mama in her room? It's about as much time as it takes to watch two of your Coma Niddy videos.*

YUKI: *OK.*

THERAPIST: *Awesome! Mama, what about you, do you think this plan makes sense?*

HIROKO: *I will do it, but I know he won't like it. He says yes now, but at home he'll be telling me not to go or holding on to me.*

THERAPIST: *I'm guessing you're right! You know him pretty well, and that's what most kids with separation anxiety would do. But here we're talking about your homework instead of his. So for this, your job will be to try to go even though he doesn't want you to. It's too hard for him to say "yes" in the moment. That's exactly why I think we need to do something like this. Precisely because for him to choose is too hard right now. But it will get easier. So here again, you're not trying to force him to do something; you're just going to do it. Don't say, "I'm going now, OK?" If you ask Yuki if it's OK, what's he going to say?*

HIROKO: *He's going to say no.*

THERAPIST: *Exactly. So don't ask. We've all agreed here, so just tell him "Mama's going for five minutes now" and then go!*

HIROKO: *What if he knocks on the door?*

THERAPIST: *What do you think you should do if he knocks?*

HIROKO: *Don't answer?*

THERAPIST: *That's what I think too. He knows where you are. And he knows why you're there. He'll be OK for five minutes. I'm sure he can handle it. It will be hard for him at first, but he's very strong and brave, right, Yuki?*

YUKI: *I don't know.*

THERAPIST: *I do! You're really strong and brave. That's why you've been trying to practice. So I'm totally sure you'll be fine for these five minutes while your mom is in her room.*

At their next session, Hiroko reported that she had been able to implement her plan to go to her room for five minutes each day. Yuki had responded initially with distress, which had made it very difficult for Hiroko to persevere. When she told Yuki she was going in her room for five minutes, he began to cry and to run to her, clearly intending to cling to her as he did during his exposures and many other times throughout the day. Hiroko had felt like she was "escaping" into her room and felt very bad that in her rush she had essentially slammed the door in his face. Yuki called to her and knocked on the door for the whole five minutes. When she came out, he held her and for the rest of the day seemed even more worried about separation than usual, which added to her uneasiness about continuing the plan. Nevertheless, the next day Hiroko again told him she was going into her room for five minutes. Yuki started crying again but did not run to her, which allowed her to enter her room more calmly and to close the door more softly. Yuki knocked a few times and called to her, but when she came out of her room, she saw that he was playing a game and felt heartened. Hiroko continued the practice each day and Yuki gradually reacted less and less.

Throughout the week, Yuki had continued to resist staying in his room by himself, however. On some days he refused to go up entirely, and on others he went to his room but then did not allow Hiroko to leave him alone, as had happened in the previous weeks. On the day before the session, Hiroko reminded Yuki about the session and said, "Don't you want to be able to tell the doctor that you did it? That would be really fun if we both did our homework this week." To her surprise, Yuki agreed with the sentiment, and she suggested he do it right away. Yuki went upstairs by himself and came down when she called him, five minutes later.

Treatment continued with a combination of cognitive-behavioral therapy and parent work focused on reducing the family accommodation. Yuki continued to improve, including agreeing to meet with the therapist without his mother present. The therapist also communicated with Yuki's school to plan for a coordinated response if Yuki should again feel overly anxious during the school day and to reduce the likelihood that Hiroko would accommodate by staying on the school grounds.

At the end of treatment Yuki no longer met criteria for separation anxiety disorder. The therapist recommended that they return for a check-in and booster session after two months and discussed with Hiroko the importance of remaining wary of becoming drawn into additional accommodations in the future.

Case Examples

Addressing Family Accommodation As Stand-Alone Treatment

12

Teenager with Social Phobia

PRESENTATION

Derek was a 16-year-old White, English-speaking boy. Derek was the second of four children and lived with his parents, Cody and Lucy, and his three siblings. Derek's parents presented with complaints relating to Derek's social anxiety and self-isolation, including missing many days of school. Derek had been referred by a psychiatrist whom he had seen twice and who, in addition to prescribing an antidepressant, had recommended psychotherapy. Derek, however, had refused to participate in the evaluation, and his parents arrived alone.

Derek spoke very little outside of the home, talking almost exclusively to only one or two other boys with whom he had been friends since the first grade. Even at home, Derek refused to speak to anyone apart from his immediate family and sometimes a grandparent. In the past, he had often voiced the concern that others were going to laugh at him or ridicule him, but more recently he refused to talk about his social anxiety at all. He frequently missed school, a problem that was exacerbated by his habit of staying up very late playing online video games until the early hours, making him very tired in the morning. When he did stay home from school, Derek was usually secluded in his bedroom, sometimes not coming out the whole day, even to eat. His parents sometimes left food for him on a tray near the room as they were concerned that otherwise he would not eat at all.

Derek did not participate in the evaluation, but his parents brought with them a recent photograph, which they had taken surreptitiously as Derek adamantly refused to be photographed. The picture showed a thin young man, of what appeared to be average height, with long hair that fell in bangs over his forehead and eyes. He was dressed in sweatpants and a loose, baggy, sweatshirt, which his parents described as his usual clothing.

Cody and Lucy accommodated Derek's anxiety in several ways, in addition to leaving him food near his room. They had completely stopped inviting guests to their home, and if Derek agreed to go anywhere outside of the home, they would always drive him, as he avoided public transportation. They tried to help him keep up with his schoolwork by getting assignments for him from teachers or peers and by writing emails to teachers for him and submitting work that he did. When Derek had to be taken somewhere, for example, to a doctor, Cody and Lucy agreed not to talk the whole time if anyone else (apart from the doctor) was nearby, not even between themselves. And if anyone came to the house looking for him, they would tell the visitor on his behalf that he was not feeling well, or sleeping, to make them go away. The family had greatly reduced the frequency with which they attended social events, and they had mostly stopped going to church. This was partly due to the discomfort they felt whenever people would inquire about Derek, asking how he was or why he had not come as well. They also took very few family photos because even if they did not try take his picture, Derek would become upset if photos were being taken.

If Derek wanted or needed something to be bought for him, Cody and Lucy would take care of it so that Derek did not have to interact with anyone from outside of the family. For example, when Derek's computer broke down and needed to be repaired, Lucy took it to the store and dealt with the repairs. And when Derek expressed a desire for any kind of food, his parents, who were happy to see signs of appetite, would make sure to pick it up for him when they went shopping.

EVALUATION

Based on the parents' report and on the assessment of the psychiatrist who had recently met with him, Derek met diagnostic criteria for social phobia. Prior testing had indicated average intelligence, and he was talented at drawing and sketching. His development had been largely unremarkable, apart from early signs of behavioral inhibition as a toddler. He made friends in the first grade and maintained friendships for many years, still being friends with two of the same children. Though he had stopped initiating social contact with those friends in recent years, Derek still sometimes agreed to meet with them and would talk to them in school about shared interests, especially online gaming. Lucy, Derek's mother, also suffered from social phobia growing up and had been significantly impaired until beginning treatment with an antidepressant, approximately 10 years earlier. Cody, Derek's father, described himself as "an introvert but not socially phobic," preferring small groups and home life to large gatherings but not feeling anxious about other people's judgement. Derek had been to a number of therapists over the years, with different degrees of impact and success, but after stopping his most recent therapy, approximately two years prior, he had declared that he was "done with therapists and done with therapy." He had remained adamant in his position ever since.

Derek's parents rated him in the clinically anxious range on both a general anxiety screening questionnaire and on a social anxiety scale. They also rated themselves as highly accommodating and indicated that the accommodation was causing them significant distress. They endorsed all the negative consequence items on the Family Accommodation Scale–Anxiety (FASA), indicating that if not accommodated, Derek appeared more distressed and anxious and also was prone to becoming angry or abusive.

The parents expressed the hope that if they could get Derek to meet with the therapist just one time, a bond could be formed, and Derek might agree to return to therapy. The therapist agreed to meet with Derek if he were willing but also suggested that pinning all hopes for improvement on the possibility of individual therapy was not wise. The history of repeated attempts at therapy, including cognitive-behavioral therapy, and Derek's current reluctance and low motivation for treatment, coupled with the high degree of family accommodation, made it unlikely that a successful therapy process would occur, explained the therapist. Instead, the therapist recommended the parents begin a course of parent-based treatment, using the SPACE Program to reduce family accommodation.

TREATMENT COURSE

The initial part of treatment focused on introducing Lucy and Cody to the rationale for parent-based work. The therapist clarified that although the work would be done through them, Derek was still "the patient," and the goal of treatment was to improve his social anxiety. The therapist explained the principles of the SPACE approach for targeting family accommodation and discussed the natural tendency of anxiety in children and teens to impact the entire family system. Next, the therapist introduced the concept of family accommodation, asking the parents to think about the ways in which Derek's anxiety had shaped their behavior.

> CODY: *What do we do differently because of his anxiety? What don't we do differently?! Everything is different. We used to have friends over all the time. Not big groups, but we had really close friends from college, and we would get together a lot, with the kids or without the kids, and now we never even see them. We've disappeared from them completely. We don't even have the grandparents over except for big holidays anymore, and I know that's not fair to his little brother and sister.*

> LUCY: *But it's really hard if they do come over. They always have something to say. My dad is old school. He'll say things like "How come I never heard about this kind of thing when I was growing up?" or they'll drop all kinds of judgements that make it obvious that we're handling it wrong. Like "Why didn't you do this?" or "You need to do that." And some of our supposed friends, parents of the other kids' friends, they don't want their kids' hanging out in our house because of him. Like he's going to scare them or make them also reclusive or I don't know what.*

> THERAPIST: *It's really painful to hear you talk about how this problem has affected your whole family. I can imagine how different it must be from the way you pictured things, from what you wanted for yourself and for Derek.*

> LUCY: *Yes . . . I never thought it would be like this. Even though I have social anxiety too, my family was much more normal. Maybe my dad's right, and we're not handling it correctly. I don't know.*

THERAPIST: *Well, it's really easy to criticize someone else when you don't actually have to handle the problem yourself. I think you're doing your best. And you being here is another thing you're doing to help Derek. And frankly, from what you've told me, it sounds like your parents might not have let your anxiety shape the family life like this, but it also sounds like you didn't get much help either. If I'm not mistaken, you said you didn't see anyone for help until you were in college.*

LUCY: *They just don't believe in mental health problems. They think it's all a matter of grit and motivation and that people like me or like Derek need a good kick up the. . . . That's pretty much what I got growing up.*

THERAPIST: *Well, I don't think that's really what's needed, and I don't think that's what you want for Derek, right? Tell me more about the family life with such an anxious boy.*

LUCY: *Well, like Cody was saying, we don't go places or do things as a family. Just planning for how to handle his sister's graduation was such an ordeal. Should we make him go? What if he won't? And what if he does? I don't even know which is worse anymore. I can't go through that kind of ordeal for things that don't matter as much, so we've just kind of stopped everything.*

THERAPIST: *I know what you mean. It's really limited you a lot. What about at home, how are things different than they might be if Derek were less anxious?*

LUCY: *We're just walking on eggshells all the time. We have to remember all the things that make him feel uncomfortable. Like not taking photographs. Or not having the TV on too loud because someone outside might hear. And leaving the food near his room. I don't know, it's like working in a nursing home instead of being in our house. And it feels like things just keep getting worse. Now we can't get him to school on lots of days. I've just sort of given up on him graduating. What am I supposed to? He's 16.*

The therapist continued to explore the different forms of family accommodation that were provided to Derek, mapping them out using a chart and "walking through" a typical day in the life of Derek and his family. Then the therapist asked Cody and Lucy to each think of a particular accommodation that they would really like to be able to stop doing. The therapist encouraged them to think about what would be most useful for Derek, but also what would make their lives better if they were no longer accommodating. The therapist clarified that they could have different perspectives and that the goal was just to come up with an area that seemed important to each of them, and they need not necessarily agree.

THERAPIST: *So, during our last session I asked each of you to think about one accommodation that you thought might be particularly important and we could consider as a focus for our next step in treatment. Did you have a chance to think about that over the week?*

CODY: *Yes, we thought about it, and we both thought of the same thing.*

THERAPIST: *OK, great, tell me what you have in mind.*

LUCY: Well, there were actually two things. One thing is not buying stuff for him anymore and letting him do that for himself. It makes us feel like we're really enabling him when we do that.

THERAPIST: That's a great point. But before we discuss what to do, why don't you tell me the other thing you thought about as well.

LUCY: OK, so the other thing was the way we always keep the TV volume on so low we can hardly hear it. Even if Derek isn't even watching or is in his room, it's like this rule that it has to be really quiet. I don't even know how he hears it sometimes, or maybe he just comes to check up on us, because if we raise it at all he'll show up and get really mad. It's aggravating for us, but it just feels really unfair to his siblings.

CODY: Yeah, I've told them they don't really have to do that, but I think they see that we do it, and they don't want him to make a fuss either so they go along. Only his older brother will turn it up, and Derek is kind of scared of him, so he won't say anything if he's watching. But if it's anyone else. . .

THERAPIST: That's also a really good suggestion. What's really interesting to me about that one is the way Derek can handle it better if it's his older brother. What do you think that means?

LUCY: That he's scared of him?

THERAPIST: Sure, that might be true. Does he have a reason to be afraid of his brother?

LUCY: Not really. I mean he's not violent or anything. He just doesn't take Derek's shit. Sorry!

THERAPIST: No problem. I think you're may be right that he's a little less brave with his brother. But what it means to me is that when he has to, Derek is able to cope with the TV being louder. He knows he can't make his brother turn it down, so he finds a way to cope with it. That's pretty important, right?

CODY: You think if he's scared of us he'll be able to cope as well?

THERAPIST: I don't think he needs to be scared of you. I think if he knows he can't control your behavior, he'll find a way to cope, that's all. And the more he does that, the better he'll get at it. So that maybe he won't feel like he really needs it so quiet at all.

CODY: OK, maybe.

THERAPIST: So, you've told me two really useful ideas. And before we decide how to proceed, I want to ask you a couple of questions about them, and some of the other things we mapped out as well, OK? Just so we make the best plan possible.

LUCY: Yes, sure.

THERAPIST: One thing you mentioned to me when we first met, but didn't really come up when we were mapping things out, was that you sometimes put food near his room. Is that something you still do?

LUCY: I haven't done that these past couple of weeks.

THERAPIST: OK, why not? Is there a reason?

LUCY: It's just he's been out of the room most days, and once I see that he's coming out I feel better about not putting the food because I know he takes *something to eat. It's when I don't see him at all that I start to worry, and I'll leave a tray for him.*

THERAPIST: *OK, that makes sense to me. So, since it's not happening a lot, it makes sense for that not to be our target problem, but I would like to encourage you not to put that tray of food while we're doing this work, OK? I think you used the phrase "It feels like working in a nursing home" when you were describing that to me, right?*

LUCY: *That's what it looks like. Or maybe a hotel hallway with the room service near the door.*

THERAPIST: *Right, and I think it probably makes Derek feel like those things as well. Like he's convalescing in a nursing home and seriously disabled, or like he's a guest in a hotel getting service to his room. And we really don't want to encourage either of those things. He's not unable to get food if he wants it so let's trust that he'll find it when he's hungry.*

LUCY: *OK, I'll try not to do that.*

CODY: *I always thought that was a bad idea.*

THERAPIST: *Well, it's really hard for a mother to think of her son not eating. That hurts. And, of course, if he really couldn't get the food by himself, it would be the right thing to do for him. But that's great, we're agreeing not to do that for now. And if you do get really worried that he won't eat, or that he's not eating, let's talk it over together and think what the best plan is, OK? Leaving a tray is one solution but not the only one. We can think of other options. But in the meantime, he's coming out and he's eating so let's just leave it at that.*

LUCY: *OK.*

THERAPIST: *One other thing I was thinking about was how much your social life has been diminished from all this anxiety. How you don't invite people over and don't even go out. I think you really need that part of your life back. So I'm wondering about that as a target as well. What do you think?*

CODY: *We actually did talk about that as well. It's something we both want. But we're really not looking forward to having people over and having to explain about him. And I don't even know if anyone still wants to spend time with us. We've been so absent.*

THERAPIST: *I understand that, but I'm sure your friends miss you. You talked about really good friends you have since college. I doubt they suddenly decided they don't want to be friends anymore. They probably think it's you that decided not to be friends because it's been so hard for you to spend time with them.*

LUCY: *That's true. My friend Eileen has messaged me to ask what's going on and why I'm never around. She even asked if I'm mad at her for something. I told her of course not, but I just didn't want to get into the whole explanation about Derek, so I left it at that.*

THERAPIST: *See, I'm sure your friends can tell that something is wrong, and they probably want to help you and support you. Isn't that how you would feel if they seemed to have a problem?*

LUCY: *Yes, of course. I would want to help.*

THERAPIST: *Exactly! So, OK, I understand if you don't want to take on having people over just yet. It may be an important step for us, but it doesn't have to be the first one, right? But how about this: While we're working on a different target, you guys start spending some time with your friends outside of home. If you want, we can think about a good way to explain Derek's problems to them so they'll understand. I doubt they will judge or criticize you like you get from your parents. I'm even happy to meet together if you wanted to invite them to join one of our sessions, and I can help to explain. But the important thing is, you start rekindling your social life just a little bit at a time. And soon, when Derek's anxiety is improving from the other work we'll do, maybe you'll be able to do more of that at home as well, deal?*

CODY: *Yes, deal. I'm kind of happy to be thinking that actually.*

LUCY: *I don't know about happy . . . but OK.*

THERAPIST: *Great, thank you! So let's get back to picking a target. You mentioned two important things: not buying things for him that he wants and not keeping the TV on so low all the time. I think they really are both good ideas, but I really like the volume idea because it just seems like something you'll be able to practice more frequently.*

CODY: *That's true. It's not like we're buying things every day.*

LUCY: *Apart from food. But I would buy food anyway I guess.*

CODY: *Plus, if we say we won't buy something, most of the time he'll just prefer not to get it than to deal with it himself. Maybe he would get the computer fixed, because that's like his whole life now. But most things he'd rather do without.*

THERAPIST: *Those are really good points too. So, the TV is something that could happen more frequently and also something that is really just up to you to do. It doesn't depend on his reaction very much, which is good because it means you can be in control.*

In the next session, the therapist and the parents developed a specific plan for how to tackle the accommodation around the television volume. They wrote an announcement that the parents would deliver to Derek before beginning to implement the plan and also discussed how to talk about their plan with the other children. They agreed to make very clear to the younger siblings that they were not expected to keep the television so low anymore but not to require them to raise the volume if they didn't choose to do so. The parents were surprised by the degree of detail the therapist required they include in their plan. For example, the therapist asked if the volume indicator on their television showed a number or a bar, and the parents had to call their eldest son who was home to find out. It turned out that the television showed a number on a scale of one to one hundred, and the therapist recommended that they agree on a specific number for how loud to make it. The therapist explained that it would be easier for them to be persistent and consistent if they knew exactly what the plan required and that it would help them to avoid becoming embroiled in argument or negotiation with Derek, or each other. Or another example: It became apparent in devising the plan that a related accommodation was to close the living room windows when the television was on to further reduce the likelihood that it could be heard from outside. The therapist suggested including explicitly in the plan that they would not close any windows because of the television, but recommended they not open them if Derek chose to close them, to avoid getting drawn in to a back and forth game of "open and close the windows."

Finally, the therapist asked Cody and Lucy how angry they thought Derek might become at their behavior and whether they had a concern that he would be physically aggressive to anyone or to their property. Both parents were confident that although Derek was likely to get very angry and perhaps would raise his voice or make threatening statements and looks, he would not actually act aggressively and would probably choose to isolate himself in his room. The therapist accepted this but discussed contingency plans for the event that things seemed to be getting out of hand. The plan was for the parents to turn off the television if Derek became physically aggressive or violent, and the therapist assured them that they would discuss this together and put in place additional tools to better cope with such events in the future, without returning to the accommodating behavior.

> CODY: *But won't that just show him that he's won? If we turn off the TV? Won't it make him act even worse the next time?*
>
> THERAPIST: *Derek may feel like he's "won" that battle, yes. But we're not fighting a war, and we don't need you to "win" all the time. There's no benefit in provoking violent behavior, and I'd rather he thinks he "won" and then have you come back with a better plan the next time and just keep going than provoke him or you to do things that are dangerous or to escalate the situation. That's the key. He'll see in time that you are willing to persist and to keep going despite his reactions, and that's more important than showing him "who's boss" when he's losing control. You'll just keep going and keep going, coming up with solutions to whatever happens, and in the end, that's how you really win, by persisting and not giving up. And you'll have won without making an enemy of him. Remember, we're doing this for you, but we're doing this mainly for him! To help him get less anxious. So if things get out of hand, just stop and tell yourself "OK, I need to think about how to handle this better next time," and you'll come back here and go home with a good plan, and keep going.*

The therapist also introduced to the parents the concept of support and coached them on making supportive statements to Derek prior to implementing the plan and in response to his distress when they raised the television volume.

The parents were able to implement the plan to watch TV at higher volume with relatively little difficulty and only minor resistance on Derek's part. They were surprised that he did not object more strongly to their plan and encouraged by what seemed like a rapid ability to adjust to the new behavior. Lucy and Cody also began to re-establish their relationships with old friends. During one of Lucy's dinner dates with a close friend she had not seen for a long time, she shared details of the difficulties that they had been having with Derek. To her surprise, the friend not only expressed empathy, rather than judgement, but also opened up about problems she faced with her own daughter. She described how her daughter had been suffering from depression for the past year and was taking medication after having been briefly hospitalized some months earlier. Lucy was overwhelmed. She felt supported by her friend and also felt strong guilt about not having been there for her during such a difficult crisis. The friend said that she had tried to reach out but had sensed that Lucy did not want to engage and had tried to respect that. Both friends agreed to try to be there more for each other, and Lucy felt emboldened enough to ask her if she would be willing to come over, despite the possibility that Derek would behave rudely during the visit. The friend was not fazed by this, and they arranged a time for the visit.

In discussing this with the therapist, the therapist expressed support for Lucy and was glad that she was able to reconnect with such a close friend. The therapist also observed that having a guest come to the house was an excellent thing for Derek but that Cody might feel left out if Lucy were to start making plans without consulting with him first. Cody acknowledged that he had been upset by this but had not wanted to interfere or to dampen his wife's happiness about resuming her friendship. The therapist planned with the parents how to inform Derek about the visit and how they would respond if he were to become angry or upset. They agreed that the friend would attempt to say hi to Derek if he were in the room but would not insist on communication beyond that and would not seek him out if he chose to be in another room.

Over the course of therapy, the parents continued to reduce their accommodating behavior and to resume their social lives, increasingly inviting people into the home. Derek's siblings also felt able to invite friends over and began doing so with regularity. Derek's older brother, whom the parents had mentioned that Derek felt "afraid of" turned out to be a very important supporter as well. He expressed to Derek that he felt proud of him for finally "letting the family live a normal life" and offered to take him out to celebrate. To everyone's surprise, Derek accepted the offer, and the two boys went out to eat.

As the accommodations diminished, Derek's social anxiety began to abate as well. The parents noticed that he no longer hid in his room when people came over, and after a few more weeks, he began to respond when spoken to. The parents also enlisted the help of Derek's two good friends, whom he had known for many years. They spoke with them about Derek's difficulty in social situations and asked them if they thought they could encourage Derek to meet more people. Both boys took on the challenge and began encouraging Derek to include additional friends in their small group. Derek was reluctant at first but agreed on the condition that he did not have to speak to anyone new. Despite this, he soon became friends with two additional youths, and the group began regularly hanging out. Derek's teachers also noted a change in his behavior, describing him as less reclusive and more social.

Derek persisted in his refusal to engage directly with therapy but became more willing again to acknowledge his social anxiety. He agreed that it was improving but still felt very worried in most social situations. He disclosed that one of his major concerns was not about saying the wrong thing but that the physical signs of his anxiety would make him appear strange or foolish. He worried that others would notice that he was blushing or trembling and that it would look ridiculous. The parents reported this to the therapist who explained this was a common symptom of social anxiety. The therapist suggested to Cody and Lucy that they ask Derek if he would be willing to learn some regulation strategies to better keep his physical anxiety under control. Derek said he did want to learn them but that he would not agree to come to therapy. The therapist suggested that the parents could learn the strategies and teach them to Derek, and this proved very helpful. The therapist also suggested some online resources Derek could use to learn additional skills, including challenging his thoughts and planning ways to practice social situations.

By the end of the parent work, the accommodations were almost entirely removed, and Derek had learned and practiced much of what would be taught in a typical course of cognitive-behavioral therapy. Cody and Lucy both agreed that Derek would never have agreed to learn those things before they removed the family accommodation. Despite some remaining social anxiety, Lucy and Cody were happy that they had been able to help Derek to a very large extent, something they had not thought possible without him attending therapy directly.

13

Extreme Accommodation of a Child with OCD and Coercive Behaviors

PRESENTATION

Cora was a 12-year-old, African American English-speaking girl, living with her single mother, Bria, and two younger sisters. Cora presented with complaints relating to intrusive thoughts and rigid rules and rituals, many of which were imposed on the entire family. Cora also had frequent motor tics, including rolling her shoulders, twisting her nose, and flexing her abdominal muscles.

Cora's thoughts and rituals were mainly related to the domains of contamination, doubt, and sensory sensitivities including strong aversion to certain sounds, smells, or tactile sensations. Cora had obsessive fears of contamination from germs or pollutants, or anything that took on a negative connotation in her thoughts, and many cleaning rituals as well as strict rules for avoiding these contaminants. She experienced persistent doubt about whether she had done things, including both things she needed to do and things she feared having done, and her doubts led to many checking rituals and to repeated questioning. Her sensory aversions caused her to avoid and "forbid" many different objects and activities including creams and lotions, many foods, and anything that produced a scraping noise.

Cora's mother Bria, as well as her two younger sisters, aged seven and nine, engaged in extensive accommodation of her symptoms, through both active participation in her rituals and through many modifications to the family's daily life. Bria described Cora as a "tyrant," saying that any defiance of her OCD rules led to extreme havoc in the household. Cora would explode with rage if she even suspected that one of her "rules" had been broken and had hit both her mother and her sisters on numerous occasions.

Because of her fears of contamination, everyone in the family would shower and change clothes immediately upon returning home. Cora had placed a hamper near the front door and the entire family would remove all their clothes in the foyer, where they hung towels on the coat hooks and then go and shower immediately, placing the towel in the bathroom hamper and using a different one for drying after the shower. They each had separate clothes for wearing outside the home and inside, and these were kept completely separate, even being washed in different laundry loads and stored on different shelves in the closets. When driving, Bria was forbidden from taking certain roads that Cora believed to be contaminated, and the car windows had to be kept closed at all times. Even when Cora was not in the car her mother did not dare to drive the "contaminated" roads, as Cora would question her closely about where she had gone and demand that she swear to the truthfulness of her report. Certain items that had taken on negative or disgusting connotations in Cora's mind were also strictly forbidden. For example, on one of the streets she viewed as contaminated there was a McDonalds, and anything with any relation to McDonalds became contaminated for her as well. Not only did nobody in the family ever eat any food from McDonalds, even without Cora there, but any picture, book, or toy with an association to the restaurant was also "out." Even unrelated objects that had some form of golden arch were labeled contaminated and forbidden in the house.

Because of her obsessive doubting, Cora engaged in many checking rituals and often demanded that her mother participate in these along with her. For example, she would check and recheck the contents of her backpack and demand that her mother confirm what she saw. Or she would check that her belongings were in place, sometimes counting and recounting the books on her shelves together with her mother to make sure she had not lost a book, and she would check that she had turned off the water or light switch many times and send her mother or sisters to check as well and confirm it for her. Cora also had doubts about possibly having done something that was either "bad" or would contaminate her, and she would spend a long time telling and retelling every moment of her day, insisting that her mother listen without interrupting and then confirm that her doubt was not correct. She also demanded that her mother and sister share many details of their day as well, to make sure they had not been exposed to a new kind of contaminant, and if she thought they had, Cora would insist on additional cleaning rituals beyond those that had become standard family practice.

EVALUATION

Cora met criteria for obsessive-compulsive disorder (OCD), as well as for chronic motor tic disorder. Her many aggressive and argumentative behaviors were clearly the result of the OCD and thus did not warrant a separate diagnosis. Cora was a good student in most classes, in particular math and science, but she had some difficulty with English and did not enjoy reading. Her physical development was normal, but she had begun speaking at a relatively late age, only saying her first words at close to two and a half years of age. Her mother had her assessed at the time, but as she was developing normally otherwise and was able to communicate well nonverbally, no intervention had been provided. Cora's speech caught up by age four, and she mastered reading, with some difficulty, in the first grade. Her mother, Bria, who was a highly educated college graduate with advanced degrees, expressed lingering concern about Cora's language abilities, but a recent evaluation had indicated no special interventions necessary, apart from additional time on written tests. In contrast, her math skills were excellent, and she was taking advanced classes in this area.

Cora began to show symptoms of OCD by age six. Bria recalled that she became frantic one day around this age because her toothbrush fell into the sink. Cora refused to use it, insisting on getting a new one and from then on always stepped away from the sink to brush and stored her brush in a travel case. She also began to excessively wash her hands around the same age and to ask her mother questions about things that could "hurt her." In the early years, Bria was often able to reassure her by simply answering her questions or promising her that something would not hurt her. Cora would say, "I trust you, so I know this won't hurt me," repeating the phrase to herself sometimes over and over. Over time, it became increasingly hard for Bria to assuage Cora's fears and her reassurance only seemed to help for a brief time, if at all. In the third grade, Bria was walking Cora to school one morning when she noticed a fence with chipped paint. She immediately covered her mouth and nose saying, "Paint chips are poison" and was so distraught that Bria ended up taking her home for the day. The next day Cora insisted on crossing the street before getting near the fence, and soon they were taking a roundabout route just to avoid walking near it. Similar events occurred again and again over the years.

Cora had worked with a therapist for one year during most of her fifth year of school and part of the sixth, and there had been some improvement. She had also been taking a combination of an antidepressant and an atypical antipsychotic since beginning the therapy. The therapist had moved away, however, and because things seemed to be going a little bit better, Bria had not sought out another therapist. Now, in the seventh grade, her symptoms had escalated dramatically over several months, with the entire family in upheaval. Cora, however, now refused to return to therapy and accused her mother of planning to hospitalize her. This thought had, in fact, occurred to Bria, who acknowledged she may have used it as a threat on one or two occasions, and no amount of reassurance convinced Bria to re-enter therapy. She consented to come to the evaluation only because her mother again used the possibility of hospitalization, saying "If you won't come to evaluation as an outpatient, there may not be a choice but to have you seen inpatient. I can't just do nothing."

Cora appeared, dressed in an odd assortment of mismatched clothes, some too large and some too small for her, and wearing a knit hat that covered all her hair, despite the weather being warm. Bria explained that because Cora felt she was coming to a "bad" place, she intended to throw away any article of clothing worn to the appointment and thus had chosen items she did not want. Cora answered the therapist's questions with brief and curt answers, and her demeanor made it clear she felt she was there under duress. She acknowledged that she had OCD but showed a labile level of insight, at times denying that any of her thoughts were irrational and other times acknowledging that they were irrational but indicating that the way to overcome the problem was for her, and her whole household, to be "free of contamination" for a period of at least one week with no exposure to any contamination whatsoever. This, she said, would solve the problem, and she would not have to worry anymore. When asked, Cora acknowledged that she had never been able to achieve even one day of feeling completely contamination free, but she attributed this mainly to her family and to school, expressing anger that she kept being put in the "wrong place" and that her count of contamination-free time was continually reset to zero.

The therapist attempted to engage Cora in making a treatment plan, even offering to think together with her about how she could better pursue her aim of removing contamination, but Cora adamantly refused to even consider coming to another session with the therapist. She did make one small concession, telling the therapist that her refusal is "not personal" and that although there was no chance she would ever agree to come back, she might be willing to possibly speak over the phone from home.

Cora and Bria both rated Cora's OCD symptoms as clinically impairing and severe, scoring respectively 32 and 36 on the Children's Yale Brown Obsessive-Compulsive Scale (CYBOCS).

The severity of the OCD, the high degree of family accommodation, and Cora's refusal to even consider therapy at this time led the therapist to suggest parent work focused on reducing family accommodation. The therapist hoped that reducing the accommodation would increase Cora's willingness to engage directly in therapy. The therapist also agreed to take Cora up on her offer of phone sessions from home to see if this could add to the treatment process.

TREATMENT COURSE

The therapist began to meet with Bria and, over several sessions, introduced the importance of reducing accommodation, sharing with her information about the role of accommodation in the course and treatment response of childhood OCD and mapping out the many different ways in which Cora was being accommodated. The therapist then coached Bria on making supportive statements and encouraged her to practice making these statements to Cora at home. Bria at first felt that the supportive statements felt phony or affected, because they did not convey the level of frustration and anger that she actually felt about all the accommodations she had been forced to make. The therapist acknowledged this feeling but pointed out that she had been making those accommodations because of her concern for Cora and because she knew that Cora truly suffered if she was refused. The supportive statements express this feeling but added to it the confidence in Cora's actual ability to cope with less accommodation. Bria was also disappointed to find that the supportive statements had very little impact on Cora's behavior, who largely brushed them aside or ignored them. The therapist reminded Bria that the goal of the supportive statements is to express support for Cora and provide a framework for the reduction in accommodation that is to follow, but that they were not likely to cause a marked change in Cora's behavior directly.

As a first target, the therapist and Bria agreed that she would stop participating in the ritual of removing all her clothes and showering when she returns home. They debated whether to reduce the accommodation gradually, by having her shower when she came home but not remove her clothes in the foyer, or to completely stop the ritual and stay in her work clothes until the evening. At first, the therapist suggested stopping the ritual completely, but Bria was concerned that if she did that Cora would not be able to feel comfortable around her the whole afternoon. Whereas if she did not remove her clothes in the foyer but did shower, Cora would have to get used to the change but would know that Bria had at least showered, and she could feel more comfortable around her. The therapist acknowledged this and, since Bria was clearly opposed to the alternative strategy, agreed they could start that way. They agreed that Bria would deliver an announcement, explaining the plan to Cora the day before the next session so that they could meet one more time before she actually implemented the plan. They also agreed that Bria would suggest that Cora could speak to the therapist that day on the phone if she chose. They did not call the therapist that day.

At the following session, Bria recounted that the announcement had gone very poorly. Cora flew into a rage as soon as she understood that Bria intended to make any changes, and when she heard the details of the plan, she became even more explosive. She yelled for a long time, slammed doors, and threw things in the house, breaking an art project her younger sister had created and damaging the hinge of a door. She accused her mother of "ruining everything" and told her she had just been starting to get better and now it would be ruined. When her mother did not respond to these accusations, she continued to yell and scream for over an hour. Finally, exhausted, she broke down and began to cry, pleading with her mother not to go ahead with the plan and promising to overcome the problem on her own if Bria would just giver her more time. When Bria tried to soothe her but did not consent to change the plan, Cora again became angry and accused her mother of not loving her, of never having loved her, and of always having preferred her sisters to her. She also said her mother's plan was just a way of trying to get her out of the house or even to kill her. Cora was so loud that a neighbor came by to ask if everything was OK, and this ultimately was what ended the outburst that night. All in all, Bria was exhausted and dispirited following the difficult announcement and extremely worried about how Cora would react to the actual change in her behavior. She also now felt that she had made a mistake by adopting the more gradual plan rather than just stopping the shower completely, because she thought Cora would not want to be with her anyway and because she did not look forward to having to repeat the process many times.

THERAPIST: *Well! That sounds just awful! You must be exhausted!*
BRIA: *I just don't know how I'm going to deal with her. Maybe this isn't something that can really be done without her. You should have seen her; it was like a monster took over her whole body. She's gotten angry a lot of times in*

the past, but this was just another level. It just went on and on. Every time I thought she was calming down, she would just set herself off again. And can you imagine, our neighbor coming to my door thinking somebody is being hurt or something. I'm glad they didn't call the police right away.

THERAPIST: *I can imagine! You'd be surprised, though. Cora's reaction is not actually out of the ordinary.*

BRIA: *You weren't there.*

THERAPIST: *Fair enough. You're right, I wasn't there. And I'm not in your shoes. Dealing with something like that. Maybe I can't imagine. But I can sympathize. And more important, I can tell you that the rule doesn't go "A strong reaction means it won't work." Not at all! Cora's reaction was truly awful. But it doesn't mean that you can't help her with this plan. I would actually take it as a sign that it is likely to help.*

BRIA: *Really? Why? Wouldn't it be a better sign if she had said "OK" or something.*

THERAPIST: *Well, if a child with that level of OCD and accommodation just said "OK" to a plan like ours, what would you guess that it means? Do you think that kid really believes anything is going to change?*

BRIA: *Maybe not.*

THERAPIST: *Definitely not. Maybe for a kid with mild symptoms or an extremely super compliant child. But a child like Cora—who has a strong will and a fierce determination? Both attributes that will serve her well in life, by the way. Not a bad thing to have fierce determination. But for a kid like that to just say, "Sure, fine, whatever" when her mom says "I'm not doing this accommodation that you rely on so much every day"? To me, that means "Sure, fine, whatever, we'll see!" as in "No way!" No, the fact that she railed against this for as long as she did tells me something very important. It tells me that, deep down, Cora knows you mean business. That she believes you have the capacity, which not every mom has by the way, to make a plan and act on it despite her objections. That's actually a big leg up for us. Usually the first couple of weeks of every plan is just convincing the child that the parent can do anything. I think with Cora we get to skip that step and that will actually make the process easier rather than harder.*

BRIA: *OK, I guess that's a good thing then. But how am I going to handle it when she goes nuts today. I'm going to come home and go to my room, and it's going to be world war three for the rest of the day. I'm worried about her sisters. Isn't this going to affect them as well?*

THERAPIST: *That's a very fair question—how are you going to handle it? And I actually think Cora has already given us the answer, though she didn't mean to. But let's talk about her sisters for a minute. I understand that you're worried about the anger and outbursts and the impact they could have on them, right?*

BRIA: *Of course I am! Haven't they already been through enough with her?*

THERAPIST: *Exactly! They have already been pretty heavily impacted by this OCD, right? I think that putting up with some excitement and discomfort to get out of having to do all these accommodations is actually a lot healthier for them then continuing to put up with it, don't you?*

BRIA: *I know, I know, I should never have let them get sucked into this the way they are. I just try to get some peace and quiet for all of us. And they're so good about it. But I know it's not fair.*

THERAPIST: *Well, it's not fair to them, but can anyone really blame you? You've been doing at least as much as them. A lot more actually. Nobody is born with the knowledge of how to react when a child has OCD. These things happen gradually, and they're good sisters who are making a choice because they want to help their sister and because they want peace and quiet just like you. So, sure it's not fair, but that doesn't mean you've done them harm. And now, here you are getting ready to take on something incredibly hard so that you and they can stop with the accommodation and to help Cora herself. So it's going to be hard, but in the end everybody wins.*

BRIA: *OK, but I'm still not sure how to handle her today. It's going to get crazy.*

THERAPIST: *It probably will, yes. Maybe not crazy, but it's going to get pretty hectic. Actually, scratch that. You know what? I suspect you're right—it's going to get crazy! But I already told you, I think Cora has given us the solution.*

BRIA: *What do you mean by that?*

THERAPIST: *Well, think about it, what's the one thing that happened that helped Cora to calm down despite your announcement and without you taking it back?*

BRIA: *Nothing! There was nothing that I did that helped at all!*

THERAPIST: *Right! Nothing that you did. OK, maybe I'm talking in riddles here. What I mean is, you're right that nothing YOU did helped. But your neighbor coming to the door made a huge difference from the sound of it.*

BRIA: *Wait, you want her to scream until the neighbor comes?*

THERAPIST: *Not at all! Yesterday it happened without your planning. But now that we know that it's such a useful tool, we don't need to wait or hope that someone comes. We can have them there from the beginning. And if you don't want it to be your neighbor, it doesn't have to be.*

BRIA: *So . . . I should have another person there to see her go nuts?*

THERAPIST: *I'm actually hoping that with another person there she won't go quite as nuts as when it's only you and her and her sisters. Would you say that Cora is usually better behaved at home or in school? At home or in public?*

BRIA: *Definitely outside and at school. She never loses control outside. People think she's an angel.*

THERAPIST: *There you go! We just need to bring a little bit of that "outside effect" into the home. Now, can you think of anyone you can call that can come home with you today? Is there anyone nearby that you trust?*

BRIA: *I guess I could call my sister?*

THERAPIST: *That sounds like a good idea. Do you get along? Have you spoken with her in the past about Cora's problems?*

BRIA: *She knows we have a problem with Cora. We're not all that close, but we used to be closer and I know she still cares.*

THERAPIST: *She sounds perfect. How about if you give her a call and ask her if she could meet you there or come with you.*

BRIA: *But what would she do?*

THERAPIST: *She doesn't have to do anything. She can just come over and be there for a while. Do you think Cora is less likely to get quite as upset as yesterday if your sister is there?*

BRIA: *She might be. I think she'd be mad at me later though.*

THERAPIST: *That's OK. Right now we need to get through these first few days. I think it could really help. How about you give her a call right now?*

BRIA: *I'd rather call after I leave here.*

THERAPIST: *Sure, that's fine. If she asks you what you want her to do you can just say, "My doctor suggested it could help if I'm not alone today because I'm making some changes that I know are going to be hard on Cora and sometimes she gets really upset." I would prepare her that Cora may still get really angry, and your sister doesn't have to try to stop her. She could try to talk to Cora, but if Cora doesn't want to talk that's OK, too. And if Cora asks why your sister came you could tell her honestly, "I was worried that you would get really upset again because I know this is hard for you, so I wanted another person here with me." Just be honest about it. She may not like it, but that doesn't mean it won't help. In fact, if possible, I would try to do it for a few days, not just today. Could be just your sister or someone else tomorrow. Whatever works best. Do you think that's OK?*

BRIA: *OK, I think I can do that. But what should I do if Cora is getting really angry anyway? Even if my sister or whoever is there?*

THERAPIST: *Well, the best thing to do is to try to not get into a fight with her. You've already done what you need to do by going straight to your room and not changing in the front hall, so there's really no point in fighting, right? Try to ignore her outburst as much as possible. You can just say calmly once or twice "I know this is really hard for you, but I'm sure you'll handle it OK." And then just stop answering altogether until she calms down. Don't argue or try to convince her you're doing the right thing. There's not much chance of convincing her of that right now. And in a sense, she's right to get mad.*

BRIA: *What do you mean?*

THERAPIST: *Well, you've been going along with her OCD for a long time. And now, without her agreement, you're suddenly changing the rules on her. She isn't getting much say in the matter, and you're the one who is making the change, not her. It's natural for her to be mad about that, especially when the change is causing her to feel bad and anxious. You're doing the right thing, and, in the end, it will help her feel better, I'm sure of it, but it's reasonable for her to be mad at you when you've handled things the other way for a long time. From her point of view you're the "aggressor" here; she's just reacting to you.*

BRIA: *I know, I feel really bad for her. She is so scared of the germs and stuff.*

THERAPIST: *She is. So, of course, she's going to get upset at you. There's no reason to be mad at her for that. Some of her behaviors are not acceptable, but it's normal for her to have this reaction. So keep that in mind, stay calm, and most important—don't get sucked in to the argument! The longer you answer or argue, the longer she'll stay mad, I guarantee it.*

BRIA: *OK.*

THERAPIST: *Great, you can send me an email this evening to tell me how it went, or you can reach me during the week if there's a problem you're not sure how to handle, OK?*

BRIA: *OK, thanks. I think I'm ready!*

Box 13.1 provides the email exchange.

At the next session, Bria was much more positive than before. She told the therapist that Cora had stopped having outbursts after the third day and that the younger sisters had also stopped changing clothes at the door. Bria wanted to remove the hamper from the foyer, but Cora herself still removed all her clothes as soon as she came in. The therapist counseled Bria to leave the hamper alone and not to attempt to interfere directly with Cora's own rituals and to maintain the focus on the accommodation instead. The rationale for not removing the hamper was that doing so could easily be construed by Cora as a provocation or an attempt to control her and could lead to a back and forth power struggle with Cora repeatedly returning the hamper to its place and Bria removing it. This kind of power-struggle is likely to lead to escalating conflict and hostility between child and parent and, importantly, is completely unnecessary to the process of reducing accommodation. By focusing on her own behavior and not trying to force a change on Cora directly, Bria would be better able to maintain her supportive stance while continuing to refrain from providing accommodation. The therapist also suggested continuing the current plan for one more week before taking the next step in reducing accommodation and to make many supportive statements praising Cora's improved coping. Bria asked if it would be appropriate to buy Cora a treat or prize or whether that would be seen as a "bribe." The therapist responded that a small treat or reward would be a very nice gesture and would remind Cora that her mother is not acting out of anger or resentment toward her. The therapist also again expressed willingness to speak on the phone with Cora (or to meet with her if she agreed), but Bria said she did not think it likely that Cora would want to talk with the therapist as she had said some "very rude things" about the treatment process and the therapist. Nonetheless, the therapist suggested Cora should be made aware that the she could speak with the therapist if she chose.

After an additional week maintaining the current level of accommodation, Bria and the therapist modified the plan. Bria would now stop the showers altogether when returning home. They planned another announcement that Bria would deliver to Cora informing her in a supportive manner of the new plan. Bria was worried that Cora would avoid contact with her and not be able to get emotional support. "She let me kiss her on that first night, but I don't think she'll let me do that if I haven't taken a shower." Bria was concerned that Cora would be "left

Box 13.1

EMAIL EXCHANGE BETWEEN PARENT AND THERAPIST

Bria Brooks 7:36 PM

Cora—Update

To: Dr. H. Stone
Hi Dr S., you said I could send an update so here goes. . . . Cora is currently in the other room shouting and crying. Not sure what I should do. My sister is here and saying maybe we need to take her to a hospital?? Having her here has helped only in that Cora is doing her outburst in her room instead of all over. What should I be doing? I understand if you can't answer right away but if you see this . . . thx.

Dr. H. Stone 8:01 PM

RE: Cora—Update

To: Bria Brooks
Hi Bria,
Thanks for updating me. It sounds like a rough evening, but not unexpected. I'm glad your sister is there and I think Cora staying in her room is an improvement. Hopefully it makes it easier for you not to get "sucked in." I would only take her to a hospital if you saw an immediate risk. Try to peek in if the door is closed and just see that she's not in physical danger. Otherwise, I would let her take the time she needs to calm down. No danger in her yelling or crying. If you do think she is in danger (or putting anyone else in physical danger) then definitely take her to an ER or call 911. But again, screaming and/or crying are not dangerous. I know it's hard but try to stay calm. Have a coffee or tea with your sister and just wait it out. You're doing great and you should be really proud of yourself. This is as a good a start as we could have hoped for, so I'm very optimistic. Feel free to keep me posted over email.

Bria Brooks 10:38 PM

RE: Cora—Update

To: Dr. H. Stone
Me again. Just letting you know that Cora has FINALLY!! calmed down and has fallen asleep. She cried for a really long time and she didn't eat any supper at all. I went in just as she was falling asleep and she let me give her a kiss. Ok, thx and sorry for bothering you so late!

Dr. H. Stone 6:42 AM

RE: Cora—Update

To: Bria Brooks
Good morning Bria. I'm glad Cora was able to fall asleep in the end and I think it's amazing she was able to get a kiss from you, that's just beautiful! And really good for you for even trying. Great way to show her you understand that this is hard for her and are not mad at her at all, and to do it without giving in to the accommodation. Nice job! I would tell her this morning that you're proud of her for getting through yesterday and coping. You can tell her how strong she is and that you love her. But I would stay away from questions about whether you will go back to the "old" rule about the clothes. If she asks you could just say one time "You know the plan, it's hard but I'm sure you'll be fine." And then try to change subject or get away from her for a bit. Good luck this afternoon, I hope someone can be there with you again. And I'm sure if you keep going this way you'll see that she's handling it much, much better real soon. You can update me again if you want, have a good day.

---

alone" because of her contamination fear. The therapist acknowledged this concern but advised Bria to make supportive gestures and to not take for granted that Cora would not want to be close to her. The therapist counseled Bria not to try to impose any kind of closeness and to respect Cora's avoidance as her prerogative but to make clear that she still wanted to give her a hug or a kiss and to talk warmly to her when Cora was not acting aggressively. The therapist also suggested again having Bria's sister or someone else there on the first days of implementing the new plan.

This goal followed a similar pattern to the first plan. Cora reacted at first with a lot of anger and distress, and even the presence of her aunt did not prevent her from yelling and throwing things in the house. However, Bria was able to remain calm and not escalate the situation. Bria had also arranged for the younger sisters to not be at home on the first day, and this made it a little bit easier for her to ignore the problematic behaviors. Once again, Cora's behaviors gradually diminished, and Bria also began to notice some improvement in Cora's own contamination rituals. She began going directly from the front door to the shower, rather than removing her clothes in the foyer, and Bria observed her touching the remote control for the television. Cora had avoided touching the remote ever since it had been temporarily lost a few months earlier, causing Cora to worry about "where it had been and what it had touched" while it was missing.

Over the rest of the therapy, Bria gradually removed one accommodation after another. Following the showering rituals, she focused on reducing accommodations relating to not driving on particular streets and not providing

Cora with daily reports about where she had driven or been. At first, Bria focused only on her behavior when Cora was not in the car and on the daily reports but ultimately was able to resume driving those routes even when Cora was with her, which she experienced as a monumental accomplishment.

Cora herself never agreed to actively participate in treatment, and the therapist had only a single brief conversation with her on the phone, which was polite and cordial but not particularly useful. However, over several months of treatment, Bria and her younger daughters discontinued most of their accommodating behavior, and Cora's own OCD symptoms improved a great deal as well. The therapist also held one session with Bria and both younger sisters, during which the therapist provided a lot of information about OCD, explaining their sister's behaviors and expressing support for the difficulty they had endured, as well as praising them for reducing the accommodation as a means of helping their older sister get better.

By the end of the regular treatment sessions (there continued to be sporadic sessions when Bria felt the need), Cora showed significant improvement, and the family functioning had improved dramatically. Cora still had several OCD symptoms, but the interference associated with these symptoms and the degree of impairment they caused was heavily reduced. At their last session, Bria again completed the CYBOCS and her rating of Cora had gone from 34 prior to treatment to 15. Cora did not agree to come in to the session, but she also completed the CYBOCS at home and scored 17, compared with 32 at the initial evaluation.

Family Accommodation Scale–Anxiety

Your name: Child's name:
Relationship to child: Child's age:
Participation in symptom related behaviors in the past month

		Never	1–3 times a month	1–2 times a week	3–6 times a week	Daily
1	How often did you reassure your child?	0	1	2	3	4
2	How often did you provide items needed because of anxiety?	0	1	2	3	4
3	How often did you participate in behaviors related to your child's anxiety?	0	1	2	3	4
4	How often did you assist your child in avoiding things that might make him/her more anxious?	0	1	2	3	4
5	Have you avoided doing things, going places or being with people because of your child's anxiety?	0	1	2	3	4

Modification of functioning during the past month

6	Have you modified your family routine because of your child's symptoms?	0	1	2	3	4
7	Have you had to do things that would usually be your child's responsibility?	0	1	2	3	4
8	Have you modified your work schedule because of your child's anxiety?	0	1	2	3	4
9	Have you modified your leisure activities because of your child's anxiety?	0	1	2	3	4

Distress and Consequences	No	Mild	Moderate	Severe	Extreme
Does helping your child in these ways cause you distress?	0	1	2	3	4
Has your child become distressed when you have not provided assistance? To what degree?	0	1	2	3	4
Has your child become angry/abusive when you have not provided assistance? To what degree?	0	1	2	3	4
Has your child's anxiety been worse when you have not provided assistance? How much worse?	0	1	2	3	4

Family Accommodation Scale–Anxiety (Child Report)

Child Name: _____ Date: _____

DIRECTIONS: *To be filled out by the child.* Parents do many different things to help their children not feel anxious (worried, nervous, or scared). Please circle the number that best describes how much your parent did the things listed <u>in the past month</u>.

		VERY RARELY	RARELY	SOME TIMES	OFTEN	VERY OFTEN
1	How often did your parent reassure you (like tell you that you don't need to worry, tell you something is ok)?	0	1	2	3	4
2	How often did your parent give you things to make you feel better because you were anxious?	0	1	2	3	4
3	How often did your parent participate in (do with you) the things you do because you feel anxious?	0	1	2	3	4
4	How often did your parent help you avoid things that make you feel anxious (like tell your teacher not to call on you in class, let you stay home from school?	0	1	2	3	4

5	How often did your parent avoid doing things, going places or being with people because of your anxiety?	0	1	2	3	4
6	How often did your parent change the family routine because of your anxiety (like changing bed time, chores, or other routines)?	0	1	2	3	4
7	How often did your parent do things for you that you were supposed to do yourself, because of your anxiety?	0	1	2	3	4
8	How often did your parent change his/her work schedule because of your anxiety?	0	1	2	3	4
9	How often did your parent change his/her fun plans because of your anxiety (like cancelling an activity because you didn't want him/her to leave)?	0	1	2	3	4

		Strongly Disagree	Disagree	Neither Agree nor Disagree	Agree	Strongly Agree
10	My parent gets upset when he/she helps me in these ways?	0	1	2	3	4
11	I get *upset* if my parent does <u>not</u> help me in these ways?	0	1	2	3	4
12	I get *angry* if my parent does <u>not</u> help me in these ways?	0	1	2	3	4
13	My anxiety gets worse when my parent does <u>not</u> help me in these ways?	0	1	2	3	4
14	When my parent helps me in these ways, I feel less anxious?	0	1	2	3	4
15	If my parent continues to help me in these ways, I will feel less anxious in the future.	0	1	2	3	4
16	I believe my parent should help me <u>less</u> in these ways, when I'm anxious.	0	1	2	3	4

REFERENCES

Adelman, C. B., & Lebowitz, E. R. (2012). Poor insight in pediatric obsessive compulsive disorder: Developmental considerations, treatment implications, and potential strategies for improving insight. *Journal of Obsessive-Compulsive and Related Disorders, 1*, 119–124. https://doi.org/10.1016/j.jocrd.2012.02.003

Barmish, A. J., & Kendall, P. C. (2005). Should parents be co-clients in cognitive-behavioral therapy for anxious youth? *Journal of Clinical Child & Adolescent Psychology, 34*, 569–581. https://doi.org/10.1207/s15374424jccp3403_12

Benito, K. G., Caporino, N. E., Frank, H. E., Ramanujam, K., Garcia, A., Freeman, J., . . . Storch, E. A. (2015). Development of the pediatric accommodation scale: reliability and validity of clinician- and parent-report measures. *Journal of Anxiety Disorders, 29*, 14–24. https://doi.org/10.1016/j.janxdis.2014.10.004

Birmaher, B., Khetarpal, S., Brent, D., Cully, M., Balach, L., Kaufman, J., & Neer, S. M. (1997). The Screen for Child Anxiety Related Emotional Disorders (SCARED): Scale construction and psychometric characteristics. *Journal of the American Academy of Child and Adolescent Psychiatry, 36*, 545–553. https://doi.org/10.1097/00004583-199704000-00018

Bögels, S. M., & Brechman-Toussaint, M. L. (2006). Family issues in child anxiety: Attachment, family functioning, parental rearing and beliefs. *Clinical Psychology Review, 26*, 834–856. https://doi.org/10.1016/j.cpr.2005.08.001

Breinholst, S., Esbjorn, B. H., Reinholdt-Dunne, M. L., & Stallard, P. (2012). CBT for the treatment of child anxiety disorders: A review of why parental involvement has not enhanced outcomes. *Journal of Anxiety Disorders, 26*, 416–424. https://doi.org/10.1016/j.janxdis.2011.12.014 22306129

Calvocoressi, L., Lewis, B., Harris, M., Trufan, S. J., Goodman, W. K., McDougle, C. J., & Price, L. H. (1995). Family accommodation in obsessive-compulsive disorder. *American Journal of Psychiatry, 152*, 441–443. https://doi.org/10.1176/ajp.152.3.441

Chu, B. C., & Kendall, P. C. (2004). Positive association of child involvement and treatment outcome within a manual-based cognitive-behavioral treatment for children with anxiety. *Journal of Consulting and Clinical Psychology, 72*, 821–829. https://doi.org/10.1037/0022-006x.72.5.821

Costello, E. J., Egger, H. L., Copeland, W., Erkanli, A., & Angold, A. (2011). The developmental epidemiology of anxiety disorders: Phenomenology, prevalence, and co-morbidity. In W. A. Silverman & A. P. Field (Eds.), *Anxiety Disorders in Children and Adolescents* (2nd ed., pp. 56–75). Cambridge, England: Cambridge University Press.

Eley, T. C., McAdams, T. A., Rijsdijk, F. V., Lichtenstein, P., Narusyte, J., Reiss, D., . . . Neiderhiser, J. M. (2015). The intergenerational transmission of anxiety: A children-of-twins study. *American Journal of Psychiatry, 172*, 630–637. https://doi.org/10.1176/appi.ajp.2015.14070818

Garcia, A. M., Sapyta, J. J., Moore, P. S., Freeman, J. B., Franklin, M. E., March, J. S., & Foa, E. B. (2010). Predictors and moderators of treatment outcome in the Pediatric Obsessive Compulsive Treatment Study (POTS I). *Journal of the American Academy of Child and Adolescent Psychiatry, 49*, 1024–1033. https://doi.org/10.1016/j.jaac.2010.06.013

Gee, D. G., Gabard-Durnam, L., Telzer, E. H., Humphreys, K. L., Goff, B., Shapiro, M., . . . Tottenham, N. (2014). Maternal buffering of human amygdala-prefrontal circuitry during childhood but not during adolescence. *Psychological Science, 25*, 2067–2078. https://doi.org/10.1177/0956797614550878

Ginsburg, G. S., Siqueland, L., Masia-Warner, C., & Hedtke, K. A. (2004). Anxiety disorders in children: Family matters. *Cognitive and Behavioral Practice, 11*, 28–43. https://doi.org/10.1016/s1077-7229(04)80005-1

Harlow, H. F. (1960). Primary affectional patterns in primates. *American Journal of Orthopsychiatry, 30*, 676–684. https://doi.org/10.1111/j.1939-0025.1960.tb02085.x

Johnco, C., Salloum, A., De Nadai, A. S., McBride, N., Crawford, E. A., Lewin, A. B., & Storch, E. A. (2015). Incidence, clinical correlates and treatment effect of rage in anxious children. *Psychiatry Research, 229*, 63–69. https://doi.org/10.1016/j.psychres.2015.07.071

Kagan, E. R., Peterman, J. S., Carper, M. M., & Kendall, P. C. (2016). Accommodation and treatment of anxious youth. *Depression and Anxiety, 33*, 840–847. https://doi.org/10.1002/da.22520

Lebowitz, E. R. (2013). Parent-based treatment for childhood and adolescent OCD. *Journal of Obsessive-Compulsive and Related Disorders, 2*, 425–431. https://doi.org/10.1016/j.jocrd.2013.08.004

Lebowitz, E. R., Leckman, J. F., Silverman, W. K., & Feldman, R. (2016). Cross-generational influences on childhood anxiety disorders: Pathways and mechanisms. *Journal of Neural Transmission, 123*, 1053–1067. https://doi.org/10.1007/s00702-016-1565-y

Lebowitz, E. R., Marin, C., Martino, A., Shimshoni, Y., & Silverman, W. K. (2019). Parent-based treatment as efficacious as cognitive behavioral therapy for childhood anxiety: A randomized noninferiority study of supportive parenting for anxious childhood emotions. *Journal of the American Academy of Child and Adolescent Psychiatry.* doi: 10.1016/j.jaac.2019.02.014

Lebowitz, E. R., Omer, H., Hermes, H., & Scahill, L. (2014). Parent training for childhood anxiety disorders: The SPACE Program. *Cognitive and Behavioral Practice, 21*, 456–469. https://doi.org/10.1016/j.cbpra.2013.10.004

Lebowitz, E. R., Omer, H., & Leckman, J. F. (2011). Coercive and disruptive behaviors in pediatric obsessive–compulsive disorder. *Depression and Anxiety, 28*, 899–905. https://doi.org/10.1002/da.20858

Lebowitz, E. R., Panza, K. E., & Bloch, M. H. (2016). Family accommodation in obsessive-compulsive and anxiety disorders: a five-year update. *Expert Review of Neurotherapeutics, 16*, 45–53. https://doi.org/10.1586/14737175.2016.1126181

Lebowitz, E. R., Scharfstein, L. A., & Jones, J. (2014). Comparing family accommodation in pediatric obsessive-compulsive disorder, anxiety disorders, and nonanxious children. *Depression and Anxiety*, *31*, 1018–1025. https://doi.org/10.1002/da.22251

Lebowitz, E. R., Scharfstein, L., & Jones, J. (2015). Child-report of family accommodation in pediatric anxiety disorders: Comparison and integration with mother-report. *Child Psychiatry & Human Development*, *46*, 501–511. https://doi.org/10.1007/s10578-014-0491-1

Lebowitz, E. R., Woolston, J., Bar-Haim, Y., Calvocoressi, L., Dauser, C., Warnick, E., . . . Leckman, J. F. (2013). Family accommodation in pediatric anxiety disorders. *Depress and Anxiety*, *30*, 47–54. https://doi.org/10.1002/da.21998

Manassis, K., Lee, T. C., Bennett, K., Zhao, X. Y., Mendlowitz, S., Duda, S., . . . Wood, J. J. (2014). Types of parental involvement in CBT with anxious youth: A preliminary meta-analysis. *Journal of Consulting and Clinical Psychology*, *82*, 1163–1172. https://doi.org/10.1037/a0036969

McGuire, J. F., Small, B. J., Lewin, A. B., Murphy, T. K., De Nadai, A. S., Phares, V., . . . Storch, E. A. (2013). Dysregulation in pediatric obsessive compulsive disorder. *Psychiatry Research*, *209*, 589–595. https://doi.org/10.1016/j.psychres.2013.04.003

Nauta, M. H., Scholing, A., Emmelkamp, P. M. G., & Minderaa, R. (2001). Cognitive-behavioural therapy for anxiety disordered children in a clinical setting: Does additional cognitive parent training enhance treatment effectiveness? *Clinical Psychology and Psychotherapy*, *8*, 330–340. https://doi.org/10.1002/cpp.314

Norman, K. R., Silverman, W. K., & Lebowitz, E. R. (2015). Family accommodation of child and adolescent anxiety: Mechanisms, assessment, and treatment. *Journal of Child and Adolescent Psychiatric Nursing*, *28*, 131–140. https://doi.org/10.1111/jcap.12116

Peris, T. S., Rozenman, M. S., Sugar, C. A., McCracken, J. T., & Piacentini, J. (2017). Targeted family intervention for complex cases of pediatric obsessive-compulsive disorder: A randomized controlled trial. *Journal of the American Academy of Child and Adolescent Psychiatry*, *56*, 1034–1042. https://doi.org/10.1016/j.jaac.2017.10.008

Pinto, A., Van Noppen, B., & Calvocoressi, L. (2013). Development and preliminary psychometric evaluation of a self-rated version of the Family Accommodation Scale for Obsessive-Compulsive Disorder. *Journal of Obsessive-Compulsive and Related Disorders*, *2*, 457–465. https://doi.org/10.1016/j.jocrd.2012.06.001

Poznanski, B., Cornacchio, D., Coxe, S., Pincus, D. B., McMakin, D. L., & Comer, J. S. (2017). The link between anxiety severity and irritability among anxious youth: Evaluating the mediating role of sleep problems. *Child Psychiatry & Human Development*, *49*, 352–359. https://doi.org/10.1007/s10578-017-0769-1

Reuman, L., & Abramowitz, J. S. (2017). Predictors of accommodation among families affected by fear-based disorders. *Child Psychiatry & Human Development*, *49*, 53–62. https://doi.org/10.1007/s10578-017-0728-x

Salloum, A., Andel, R., Lewin, A. B., Johnco, C., McBride, N. M., & Storch, E. A. (2018). Family accommodation as a predictor of cognitive-behavioral treatment outcome for childhood anxiety. *Families in Society*, *99*, 45–55. https://doi.org/10.1177/1044389418756326

Seligman, M. E. P. (1971). Phobias and preparedness. *Behavior Therapy*, 2, 307–320. https://doi.org/10.1016/S0005-7894(71)80064-3

Settipani, C. A. (2015). The effect of child distress on maternal accommodation of anxiety: Relations with mother and child factors. *Dissertation Abstracts International: Section B: The Sciences and Engineering, 76*(2-B(E)).

Stewart, S. E., Hu, Y. P., Hezel, D. M., Proujansky, R., Lamstein, A., Walsh, C., . . . Pauls, D. L. (2011). Development and psychometric properties of the OCD Family Functioning (OFF) Scale. *Journal of Family Psychology, 25*, 434–443. https://doi.org/10.1037/a0023735

Stoddard, J., Stringaris, A., Brotman, M. A., Montville, D., Pine, D. S., & Leibenluft, E. (2014). Irritability in child and adolescent anxiety disorders. *Depression and Anxiety, 31*, 566–573. https://doi.org/10.1002/da.22151

Storch, E. A., Geffken, G. R., Merlo, L. J., Jacob, M. L., Murphy, T. K., Goodman, W. K., . . . Grabill, K. (2007). Family accommodation in pediatric obsessive-compulsive disorder. *Journal of Clinical Child & Adolescent Psychology, 36*, 207–216. https://doi.org/10.1080/15374410701277929

Storch, E. A., Salloum, A., Johnco, C., Dane, B. F., Crawford, E. A., King, M. A., . . . Lewin, A. B. (2015). Phenomenology and clinical correlates of family accommodation in pediatric anxiety disorders. *Journal of Anxiety Disorders, 35*, 75–81. https://doi.org/10.1016/j.janxdis.2015.09.001

Taylor, J. H., Lebowitz, E. R., Jakubovski, E., Coughlin, C. G., Silverman, W. K., & Bloch, M. H. (2018). Monotherapy insufficient in severe anxiety? Predictors and moderators in the child/adolescent anxiety multimodal study. *Journal of Clinical Child & Adolescent Psychology, 47*, 266–281. https://doi.org/10.1080/15374416.2017.1371028

Thompson-Hollands, J., Kerns, C. E., Pincus, D. B., & Comer, J. S. (2014). Parental accommodation of child anxiety and related symptoms: Range, impact, and correlates. *Journal of Anxiety Disorders, 28*, 765–773. https://doi.org/10.1016/j.janxdis.2014.09.007 25261837

Wood, J. J., McLeod, B. D., Sigman, M., Hwang, W. C., & Chu, B. C. (2003). Parenting and childhood anxiety: Theory, empirical findings, and future directions. *Journal of Child Psychology and Psychiatry, 44*, 134–151. https://doi.org/10.1111/1469-7610.00106

Page references to boxes and figures and tables are indicated by *b's, f's,* and *t's* respectively.
For the benefit of digital users, indexed terms that span two pages (e.g., 52–53) may, on occasion, appear on only one of those pages.

Printed in the USA/Agawam, MA
September 11, 2019

738201.006